Routledge Revivals

Feminism in Greek Literature

First published in 1923, *Feminism in Greek Literature* explores the representation of women in ancient Greek literature. It provides an in-depth analysis of various works of literature, including epic poems, tragedies, and philosophical texts, and examines how women were portrayed in these works. The book also discusses the role of women in Greek society and the ways in which literary representations of women may have reflected or influenced social attitudes towards women. It brings themes like early epic; the Ionians and Hesiod; Athens in the fifth century; Euripides and the four feminist plays; Socratic Circle; Plato, Attic Orators and Aristotle. This is an important historical reference for scholars and researchers of Greek literature, Greek history, and feminist literature.

Feminism in Greek Literature

From Homer to Aristotle

F. A. Wright

First published in 1923
by George Routledge & Sons Ltd.

This edition first published in 2024 by Routledge
4 Park Square, Milton Park, Abingdon, Oxon, OX14 4RN

and by Routledge
605 Third Avenue, New York, NY 10017

Routledge is an imprint of the Taylor & Francis Group, an informa business

Publisher's Note
The publisher has gone to great lengths to ensure the quality of this reprint but points out that some imperfections in the original copies may be apparent.

Disclaimer
The publisher has made every effort to trace copyright holders and welcomes correspondence from those they have been unable to contact.

A Library of Congress record exists under LCCN: 23013829

ISBN: 978-1-032-82820-6 (hbk)
ISBN: 978-1-003-50644-7 (ebk)
ISBN: 978-1-032-82821-3 (pbk)

Book DOI 10.4324/9781003506447

FEMINISM IN GREEK LITERATURE

FROM HOMER TO ARISTOTLE

BY

F. A. WRIGHT

LONDON
GEORGE ROUTLEDGE & SONS, LTD.
NEW YORK: E. P. DUTTON & CO.
1923

Printed in Great Britain by MACKAYS LTD., Chatham.

MANIBUS

A. W. VERRALL

ΤΡΟΦΕΙΑ

CONTENTS

INTRODUCTION

THERE is a question sometimes put to scholars, a doubt often latent in scholars' minds—How was it that Greek civilisation, with all its high ideals and achievements, fell so easily before what seems at first sight an altogether inferior culture? The difficulty is not solved by a reference to military resources or administrative skill, for moral strength is the only thing that matters in history, and a nation has never yet succeeded merely by pure intellect or by brute force. The fact is—and it is as well to state it plainly—that the Greek world perished from one main cause, a low ideal of womanhood and a degradation of women which found expression both in literature and in social life. The position of women and the position of slaves—for the two classes went together—were the canker-spots which, left unhealed, brought about the decay first of Athens and then of Greece.

For many centuries in Ionia and Athens there was an almost open state of sex-war. At Miletus a woman never sat at table with her husband, for he was the enemy with whom bread must not be broken ;

at Athens, while all the men went free, women were kept as slaves, and a stranger in the harem might be killed at sight. The sexes were sharply separated: men and women had but few opportunities for mutual esteem and affection, and domestic life—the life of the home, the wife and the children—was poisoned at its source.

The causes and results of this war, far worse than any faction or civil strife, are lamentable enough: its manifestations in ancient literature are perhaps even more important, for it is hard to say how far current opinions of feminine disabilities are not unconsciously due to the long line of writers, Greek and Latin, from Simonides of Amorgos, in the seventh century before Christ, to Juvenal in the second century of our era, who used all their powers of rhetoric and literary skill to disparage and depreciate womankind. In the whole deplorable business men were in the wrong, and they therefore took the aggressive. They applied to women the comforting doctrine of Aristotle, that some people were slaves because they were made by nature to be slaves: women were men's moral inferiors, and therefore it was men's duty to keep them down.

At Sparta certainly, and perhaps in North Greece, women occupied a very different place. Spartan women were regarded as free human beings, and the relations between the sexes were inestimably better than at Athens. But Sparta, Thessaly, Macedonia, have no direct representation in Greek literature; we get their point of view only in the writings of some Athenians, such as Plato and Xenophon, who rebelled against the current institutions of their state, and in the Alexandrian poets, Apollonius and Theocritus, who, even in the midst of the luxurious city, kept some of the freshness of their native hills. Most of the great writers came from Ionia or from Athens: the Ionians are nearly all misogynists, and have succeeded in colouring many parts of the Homeric poems with their perverse immorality: the typical Athenian, and those foreigners who found their ideal in Athens—Herodotus, Sophocles, Thucydides, the Orators—usually treat women as a negligible quantity.

Æschylus was an original thinker, and in this, as in many ways, took a different view from most of his countrymen. But it is not until we come to Euripides that we get the woman's side of the case definitely stated. Euripides ventured to doubt man's infallibility: he put the doctrine of the nobility of man, as he put the other doctrines of the nobility of race and the nobility of war, to the touchstone of a really critical intelligence, and he came to a conclusion very different from that which is expressed by the great majority of his predecessors.

Upon his own generation Euripides had a profound effect. Socrates, Aristophanes, Plato, and Xenophon are all feminists in varying degrees, and a fairly full statement of feminist doctrine may be found in their works. But the idealist did not win the day. It is true that women were never so degraded—in European civilisation at least—after Euripides' time as they had been before; but his teaching did not bear its full fruit. Aristotle—the supreme type of the practical mind—threw all the weight of his unexampled influence into the other scale, and the Aristotelian view of the natural inferiority of women prevailed: so that the poets of Ionia, libertines and profligates as most of them were, find their work completed by the philosopher of Stagirus.

Greek is the source from which most Roman writers drew their inspiration, and although the position of the Roman matron, honoured as the mother of the household, was infinitely higher than that of the too-often childless Athenian wife, there is still an undercurrent of misogyny which permeates Latin literature, and finds its fullest expression in Juvenal. All the venom of earlier writers is collected by the satirist, who adds the bitterness of his own bile, seasoned with the highly-coloured rhetoric which the Romans loved, and finally, with infinite zest, disgorges the mixture in the six hundred lines of the Sixth Satire. But, even as Aristotle sums up the final tendencies of Greek literature, so Juvenal represents almost the last effort of the anti-feminist school at Rome. The Christianity of the East and the romance of the North were already beginning to modify the grosser realism of the Mediterranean world, and towards the end of the second century the reaction came, when the Greek genius gave to the world the last, and perhaps the most fruitful, of all its gifts in literature—the romantic novel. Longus, in the *Daphnis and Chloe*, strikes a new note, and his hero is, perhaps, the first gentleman in matters of the affections that we find in ancient literature. The barbarian invasions soon came to devastate the land, but Longus had sown the seed, and he is the true father of all the love romances of mediæval chivalry. As Nausicaa is the first, so Chloe is almost the last of ancient heroines; and Greek literature, by a curious turn of fate, ironical enough considering its general tendency, ends as it begins, with the praise of the perfect maiden.

I.—The Early Epic

Any discussion of Greek literature must begin with Homer, although as regards women and the social position the Epic in its first form stands somewhat aloof from the general current of ancient thought. The Homeric poems are in a very real sense the Greek Bible, for they represent a standard of morality which in many respects is far higher than that which prevailed at Athens in the great era of Greek history, and they picture a state of society very different from the complex civilisation of the city-state.

It must be remembered that the Homeric poems were not written to suit the taste of the old Mediterranean people, who, if we may trust the evidence of archæology and certain signs in their language, had but a low code of sexual morality, and were inclined to regard women as mere instruments of pleasure. The Epic, in its original shape, was composed for the Achæan chiefs who came down into Greece from Central Europe, and in sexual matters were rather of the Scandinavian type. But the Achæans were only a small ruling class, and were soon assimilated by the conquered peoples, whose language they adopted. A second tide of invasion by the northern tribes called Dorian led to somewhat more permanent results, but the original Mediterranean race was always far superior in numbers, and unless inter-marriage was prohibited by law it was only a matter of time for the primary racial type to reappear. Hence the interest of Greek history, which is one long process of inter-blending and change: the renascence of the conquered and the gradual disappearance of the conquerors. Hence also the difference of view in all feminist matters between Homer and much of the later Greek literature.

The Odyssey especially, which, though perhaps later in composition than the original Iliad, has been less worked over and received fewer additions, is based on an entirely different idea of woman's position from that which was held after the seventh century B.C. Samuel Butler's theory that the Odyssey was composed by a woman, perhaps Nausicaa herself, is hardly capable of exact proof, but at any rate women in the Odyssey are never degraded as they are in many of the later passages of the Iliad, and the one lewd passage, the first lay of Demodocus (in Book 8), 'the loves of Ares and Aphrodite,' is a plain interpolation, and a clumsy one at that. Women indeed pull the strings in the

Odyssey: the goddess Athena, the nymphs, Calypso and Circe, and the mortals, Penelope and Nausicaa, are the principal actors in the drama. With both these latter there are traces of the old German custom of Mutterrecht: the kingship of the tribe seems to go on the woman's side. The claimants to Odysseus' chieftainship seek it through his wife; Nausicaa is the only daughter, and her marriage is of importance to all the tribe. So Calypso and Circe are represented as island-queens, living in independent sovereignty, and normally unconcerned with male companionship. Odysseus is to both very much in the position of a prince consort, and, being an active man, suffers severely from lack of occupation and lack of power. Athena is the guiding spirit of the whole action, and takes a motherly interest in the hero, but otherwise she is pure intelligence superior to man and quite free from any desire for man's society.

The women of the Odyssey follow her lead, and have little trace of that over-sexuality which is ascribed by later writers to all women as a natural trait. It cannot be said that the wise Penelope shows any womanish weakness in her constant love: she bears her husband's absence with resignation, and maintains his authority intact during a period of twenty years. On his return she is by no means over-anxious to recognise him. When the nurse tells her of the slaughter of the suitors by Odysseus she calls her a fool, and threatens her with punishment for disturbing a busy woman with idle tales. Telemachus chides her for her wilful stubbornness: Odysseus dresses himself in royal raiment, but fails to make any impression, and finally, in disgust, calls to the nurse to make him up a bed so that he may go off and sleep by himself, for, says he, this woman has a heart of iron in her breast. When at last she is convinced, she explains that her hesitation has been due to a well-founded distrust of men and their wiles, and she is content to let her husband go off the very next morning to visit the old Laertes.

Again, Nausicaa has no traces of the timid shyness which is counted a virtue among harem women. She faces the half-naked Odysseus boldly, as he comes from the bush where he has been hiding 'like a lion of the hills, rained upon and buffeted by the wind, and his eyes are ablaze,' and in all her dealings with him she is a charming mixture of generosity and caution.

Moreover, the morality of the Odyssey in all sexual matters is very high, and, if it is not offensive to say so, it is women's morality. There is very little appeal to the sensual man, and although Calypso and Circe were by later writers taken as types of the voluptuous female, their fascination in the Odyssey is left entirely to the imagination, and they are pictured as industrious housewives. The description is the same for both—'singing in a sweet voice within doors as she walked to and fro before the loom.' Little or nothing is said of any physical attraction they may have possessed.

So with the punishment meted out at the end of the story to the maid-servants who had accepted the embraces of the suitors. First, they carry out the corpses of their dead lovers, then they wash and cleanse the bloody floor, and finally they are hanged —twelve of them together—'like thrushes or doves caught in a snare; and they struggled with their feet for a little while, but not for long.' It is one of the few ruthless passages in the poem: there is no tendency here to err on the side of indulgence to the sins of the flesh, and for such sins harsher measure is dealt out to the woman than to the man.

But as significant as anything of the gulf between the Odyssey and later Greek literature is the treatment of the two famous sisters, Helen and Clytemnestra.

Helen, to the later Greeks the type of the wanton, appears in the Odyssey as the faithful wife, respected and self-respecting, of King Menelaus. She lives in his palace, busy with domestic duties, and when she thinks of the past it is to rejoice over her return home and escape from Troy, 'where,' she says, 'I used to mourn over the cruel fate which Aphrodite sent upon me, when she led me from my beloved country, leaving behind me my daughter, my home, and my husband dear, who lacked nothing of perfection in mind or in body.' It is a very different picture from that of Paris' mistress, as we have her in later stories, flying with a foreign youth from her lawful lord, and betraying her too fond master.

So Clytemnestra—after the lyric poets of the seventh and sixth centuries had worked up her story—is that most dreadful figure to King Man, the regicide, the woman who dares, by craft and guile, to kill the man set over her as ruler. In all the later stories it is Clytemnestra who arranges the details of Agamemnon's death—the bath, the enveloping robe, and the axe; it is she who deals the fatal blow, while her lover, Ægisthus, is a cowardly nonentity, entirely under the dominion of the woman.

But in the Odyssey the story is very different. It is told twice—by Agamemnon to Odysseus in Hades, and by Nestor to Telemachus at Pylos, and this last version is significant enough to be given word for word:

We Greeks (says Nestor) were lingering over there at Troy, and many a task did we fulfil. But he—Ægisthus—at his ease in the quiet valleys of Argos, where the horses feed, tried to beguile the wife of Agamemnon with soft words. At first, of course, fair Clytemnestra refused to do the shameful thing, for she was a woman of honest heart. Moreover, there was with her a minstrel, whom Agamemnon, when he went to Troy, had bidden to protect his wife. But soon the fate of heaven encompassed the minstrel, and brought him to his death, for Ægisthus took him to a desert island and left him there, a prey for the birds to tear asunder. As for the queen—he willing and she willing—he led her to his house. And many a sacrifice did he offer to the gods when he had done that great deed, which never in his heart had he expected to accomplish.

Such is the passage, and the last two sentences are a literal translation of the lines which appear thus in Pope's version :

> Then virtue was no more : her guard away,
> She fell, to lust a voluntary prey.
> Even to the temple stalked the adulterous spouse
> With impious thanks and mockery of vows.

For these are the dangers of poetical translation.

But more important than any single character or episode is the general impression given by the whole poem, and it may fairly be said that the entire framework of the Odyssey presupposes a condition of society in which women are regarded as not in the least, *quâ* women, inferior to men.

In the Iliad things are different, and the poem, as we have it now, gives us three distinct pictures of women's position in life. The original epic, the 'Wrath of Achilles' has hardly any place for women at all. It is true that Achilles' anger has for its cause the woman Briseis; but Achilles is angry, not at the loss of a woman whom he loves, but at the loss of a piece of property which he knows by experience to be of considerable value and service. Briseis is a slave—a thing, not a person. In the whole Iliad she is only mentioned ten times, and nine times out of those ten she is merely catalogued as an article of value, with the slave-dealer's epithet, 'fair-cheeked,' attached.

But this is hardly surprising. All the earlier portions of the Iliad are primarily lays of battle. They are anti-social, and woman has no part or lot in them.

The Iliad however, is built up of many different strata, and one stratum—by no means the least important—was contributed by a poet who understood and sympathised with women. In thought and language he has many affinities with the author of the Odyssey, and he is probably responsible for the one passage in the poem where Briseis appears as a human being, and makes lament over the dead body of Patroclus: a speech which served Ovid as the groundwork wherefrom—with many embellishments—he expands the letter in 'the Heroines.' From the same hand as Briseis' speech comes the supreme scene of the parting between Hector and Andromache, and all the closing passages of the Iliad: the ransoming of Hector, and the lamentation of the women—his wife, his mother, and Helen—over the corpse.

No one can read the Iliad without feeling that the moral spirit of all these passages is of a very different and of a very much higher quality than the brutality of the earliest lays, and the loose cynicism of the last additions to the poem, which we shall have next to consider.

II.—The Ionians and Hesiod

Between the Homeric poems in their first shape and the next stage of Greek literature there is a gap of centuries, and when the curtain goes up again on Greek history at the end of the eighth century, the centre of civilisation is in Asia Minor, the coast towns and their adjacent islands.

The period of fighting, invasions, and tribal migrations is over: there has been a revival of the old Minoan culture, the Greeks have become a nation of traders living in luxurious cities, such as Miletus and Mytilene. Politically they are dependent on the great Eastern land empires, and from the East they have taken ideas which vitally affect the position of women.

The first of these may be stated thus: a woman, even a free-born woman, is the property of the man who is her husband. The second, which follows from this, is that, love between man and his property being absurd, romantic affection is only conceivable between men; between man and woman it is impossible. Of these two ideas, the first, which involved the seclusion of women and the harem system, was only partially applied in ancient Greece. It flourished in Ionia and at Athens during the great period of her history, but it never took root in Sparta, or in the chief cities of Hellenistic civilisation. Its corollary, however, spread fatally from Asia to Greece, and from Greece to Italy. It lasted for many centuries, and tended to destroy all romantic love between the two sexes, and very often all the ordinary comfortable affection which may exist without romance between husband and wife. The sexes drew apart: the man, immersed in war and politics and absent from his home most of his life, had little experience of woman as a thinking animal, and unfamiliarity bred contempt. As happened again later in the world's history under the very different conditions of monastic life, the natural social intercourse between men and women was artificially hampered, and the inevitable crop of errors and perversions followed. But the monks, in their dislike of women, were at least ostensibly inspired by a strict code of sexual morality: a good deal of Ionian literature has for one of its objects a desire to defend the perverted sexual instinct which was the curse of ancient life. Of this sort are the stories of Ganymede, the young Asiatic, taken up to heaven by the ruler of the sky and displacing the maiden Hebe, and of Hylas, the minion of Heracles, whose beauty brought him to his death,

Narcissus and Hyacinthus are persons of the same type, while the heroes of this kind of literature, Jason, Heracles, and Theseus, reserve all their finer chivalrous feelings for men, and regard women as a kind of booty, to be won, if possible, by fraud; if fraud is ineffective, by the judicious use of force. Jason deserts Medea in favour of a younger and richer woman. Heracles leaves his wife, to roam abroad, capturing by force any woman that pleases him. Theseus spends his life in betraying women, and in his old age marries Phaedra, the young sister of Ariadne. But their exploits do not at all detract from the heroic character of the three worthies, for it is now recognised that women are vile creatures who deserve vile treatment, and so we have a second class of tale invented to illustrate the innate viciousness of the female sex. There is the story of Pasiphaë and the Minotaur, Myrrha and Adonis, Leda and the swan, Europa and the bull—and so on, and so on.

The same frame of mind that invented these tales ascribed to Sappho all kinds of unnatural vice, degraded Helen into a wanton, and Penelopë into a shrew, and made it seem only logical that women, being the creatures they were, should be kept prisoners in a harem and confined to child-bearing—that indispensable function being, indeed, the main reason for their being allowed to exist at all.

The tales of Pasiphaë, Leda, and Europa, however, though useful enough in their way, are a little crude, and we have a more artistic method employed in the passages which about this time were incorporated into the Iliad by Ionian poets, with the idea of degrading the whole conception of the two divinities who represent womanly love, Hera and Aphrodite. Hera, the goddess of married life, the wife in her divine aspect, is represented by these decadents as an interfering termagant, spying upon her husband and seeking always to thwart him in the enjoyment of his legitimate lusts and caprices; Aphrodite, the goddess of unrestrained physical passion, becomes a calculating courtesan.

The method pursued is that same kind of false realism which has supplied our comic stage with the well-worn themes of the old maid and the mother-in law, and it need hardly be said that it harmonises very badly with the romantic splendour of the epic lays. The heroic hexameter gives for our ears an air of nobility even to this stuff, but in its essence it is colloquial style of a rather tawdry sort, and one or two passages will illustrate its character; for example, the last hundred lines of Book I. of the Iliad, an episode altogether out of harmony with the rest of the book. Thetis has come to ask Zeus to avenge her son: Hera knows of her visit, and this is the language she uses to her husband :

> You crafty one—you know it's true ; who of the gods, pray, has been plotting with you again ? You know that is what you like, to get away from me and to make up your mind without me, keeping your plans secret : never yet have you had the decency to tell me outright what you mean to do.

Her husband, being a male, is far more reasonable in his tone : 'You must not expect to know all my business, my dear : it would be too hard for you, you know, though you are my wife,' and so on, gently putting her in her inferior place. But Hera refuses to listen to reason : 'What do you mean by that ? ' she cries. 'I have been only too ready in the past not to ask questions, I have left you at your ease, you have done what you liked,' and she proceeds to disclose her well-founded suspicions, until Zeus, giving up any further appeals to her better feelings, tells her bluntly to sit still and do what she is told. If not, 'All the gods in heaven, you know, won't be of any use to you when I come close and lay my irresistible hands upon you.' A further edifying touch is given by the well-meant intervention of Hera's lame son, Hephaestus, and the scene closes with the unquenchable laughter of the blessed gods.

Another similar episode is the passage in Book 14,

known as 'the beguiling of Zeus,' or, as we might say, 'the tricked husband.' Hera, it begins, saw her husband sitting on Mount Ida, and abhorred the sight of him. The story can be condensed by omitting all the ornamental epithets and turns of phrase which are used to give a very un-epic passage an epic colouring, and it runs somewhat like this.

Though she detests her lord, she still has to consider how to get the better of him, and she decides to dress herself in her finest. She goes accordingly to her bower, with its close-shut doors and its secret key, fastens the bolt, and begins an elaborate toilet. It is a sure sign of the odalisque that perfumes, jewellery, adornment of every kind are lavished upon her by the very men who really regard her as a chattel, and the whole description that follows reads like a passage in the *Arabian Nights*, themselves probably a product of the same kind of Greek genius as composed these portions of the Iliad. Every detail is lovingly dwelt upon; first with 'ambrosia' (the author hardly troubles himself about what ambrosia really is, and uses it as a sort of trade word), she washes her lovely skin, and then she anoints herself with oil, an 'extra-ambrosial' sort, which has been specially perfumed for her: then she combs her hair and twists it into bright, beautiful, 'ambrosial' curls. Next comes the 'ambrosial' robe with dainty patterns upon it, pinned across the chest by golden brooches, and the corset belt with its hundred tassels, and finally the earrings shining brightly with their three pendants. The goddess is now ready, except for the last two articles of a Greek lady's toilette, the yashmak veil and the sandals, and as she is going abroad she puts them on and calls upon Aphrodite. Being a woman, she begins with a circumlocution. 'Dear child,' she says, 'I wonder whether you will say yes or no to what I have to ask.' Aphrodite invites her to be a little more plain, and 'the crafty' Hera then enters into an elaborate and entirely false explanation. She wants to borrow the magic cestus of Aphrodite in order to reconcile Oceanus and mother Tethys, a pair whose matrimonial affairs have been going so badly that they are now occupying separate rooms. 'If I could only get them together,' she says, 'they would ever afterwards call me their friend.'

Whether Aphrodite believes the story or not is best left unsaid, but she at once consents: 'It is not possible or proper to refuse you, for you sleep in the arms of the mighty Zeus,' and she hands her the cestus with all its magic powers—'in it are love and desire and sweet dalliance and alluring words, which rob even the wise of their wits'—then with mutual smiles they separate.

All through the passage it will be noticed there is

a good deal of talk about magic, the same sort of magic as we get in the *Arabian Nights*, but the effect of the cestus is really quite independent of any supernatural aid. It was an article such as may be seen to-day advertised in a fashion paper—a 'soutien-gorge'—and it produced that development of the female bust and general appearance of embonpoint, which has always seemed to Eastern nations the ideal of feminine beauty.

Binding the cestus then under her breast, Hera goes off to pay her next visit, to the god Sleep, whom she begs to send Zeus into a deep slumber. For this service she promises the god 'a beautiful golden chair, something quite unbreakable, with a footstool attached.' But Sleep raises difficulties. He has tried a similar trick on Zeus before at the lady's request, and when the god awoke he was very violent, and Sleep would have been thrown out of heaven into the sea had not mother Night interfered to save him. In fine, a chair, even a golden chair, is not a sufficient reward for such a dangerous task. Hera accordingly raises her offer from a chair to a woman, and promises him one of the younger Graces as his bed-fellow. Sleep at this agrees to help, the pair go to Mount Ida, Sleep changes himself into a bird to watch the scene of beguiling, and Hera reveals herself to Zeus.

As soon as the god sees her, he asks where she is

going, and she repeats again the story of Oceanus and Tethys' misadventures and her projected intervention. But the god tells her brusquely, like a real master of the harem, that he needs her presence and that she can go there another day: then, as a climax of good taste, he recites the long list of his mistresses, beginning with Ixion's wife and ending with Leto. To this impassioned love-making, worthy of Don Juan himself, Hera, 'the crafty,' replies at first with an affectation of modesty, but the scene ends with the god in her arms: her purpose is accomplished and man once again is beguiled.

Dr. Leaf finds the passage full of 'healthy sensuousness,' but to other readers it may well seem thoroughly unpleasant, both in its sentiment and its language—for example, the horrible reiteration of TOI, 'mon chéri,' at the end of Hera's speech of invitation. Still, it is a valuable document. The brutal god and the crafty goddess are plainly the poet's ideals of man and woman; and his ideals are very low.

These two passages from the Iliad may serve as specimens of the second method of attack, that of sarcastic depreciation under the guise of realism, of which we have some further examples in Hesiod.

The strange medley that now bears his name is in the same position as the Iliad. There is much ancient wisdom, in which woman has little part.

'Get first a house, and then a woman, and then a ploughing ox,' and there are also many passages plainly inspired by the new Ionian spirit.

The few facts that we know of Hesiod's life would suggest that he was an Ionian poet who migrated to Bœotia, and incorporated into his verse the ancient lore of the country, much of it as old as anything we have in Greek literature.

Hesiod's father was a merchant who lived at Kyme, on the coast of Asia Minor. The son passed most of his life at Askra, but of his life we know little, of his death a good deal. He had a friend, a citizen of Miletus, who came to stay with him in Greece. The two Ionians travelling together were entertained by one Phegeus, a citizen of Locris. They repaid his hospitality by seducing his daughter: the girl committed suicide, and her brothers, taking the law into their own hands, avenged her ruin by killing both Hesiod and his friend, who indeed was said to have been the chief culprit.

This tale, which is by far the best-authenticated fact in Hesiod's life, does not give us a very pleasant impression as to the poet's capacity for passing judgment on women, and probably the details of the Pandora myth are his own invention. The story itself is very old, but, as told by Hesiod, it has all the sham epic machinery, while it is linked on to the ancient fable of Prometheus.

To revenge the gift of fire to men, Zeus resolves to make a woman. 'I will give them an evil thing,' he says; 'every man in his heart will rejoice therein and hug his own misfortune.' Accordingly, Hephaestus mixes the paste and fashions the doll. Athena gives her skill in weaving, Aphrodite 'sheds charm about her head and baleful desire and passion that eats away the strength of men.' Finally, Hermes gives her 'a dog's shameless mind and thieving ways.' Then the doll is dressed with kirtle and girdle, chains of gold are hung about her body, spring flowers put upon her head, and she is sent down to earth. 'A sheer and hopeless delusion, to be the bane of men who work for their bread.'

Epimetheus takes her to wife, and when he had got her, 'then and then only did he know the evil thing he possessed.' So the tale of Pandora ends, and the story of the Jar, although it comes next in the 'Works and Days,' is not certainly connected with her history. It is 'a woman,' but not necessarily Pandora, who takes the lid from the Jar of Evil Things and lets them fly free over the world, so that only one curse now remains constant.

That curse, it will be remembered, is Elpis—not so much Hope as the gambler's belief in Luck. It is the idea that things must change for the better if you will only risk all your fortune: that the laws of the universe will be providentially altered for your benefit; the belief, in fact, that so often makes the elderly misogynist take a young wife.

Such is Hesiod's attitude towards women, and with Hesiod the first stage of Greek literature comes to an end.

III.—The Lyric Poets

Of the literature of the seventh and sixth centuries before Christ, the lyric, iambic and elegiac poetry, we have only inconsiderable fragments. There are two reasons for the disappearance. In the case of the greatest names, Alcæus and Sappho, the Romans preferred the adaptations of Horace to the originals. With most of the other poets, the general standard of morality in their verse is so low that they fell under the ban of the Early Church, and as we know—unreasonably enough in her case —Sappho was included with them, and her poems publicly burnt. But in the fragments that we do possess there appears unmistakably the same mixture of sensual desire and cynical distaste for women which disfigures the late Epic; until in this period it ends in sheer misogyny.

In nothing is Aristotle's great doctrine of the golden mean more valuable than in matters of sex. The sexual appetite is as natural as the appetites of eating and drinking; and as necessary for that which is nature's sole concern, the preservation of the species. If the sexual appetite is wholly starved, the result is as disastrous to the race as the total deprivation of food and drink would be to the individual: if it is unduly fostered, Nature revenges herself in the same way as she does upon those who exceed in the matter of food or drink, and abnormal perversities of every kind begin. In sex matters the normal man and woman alone should be considered —the father and the mother of a family—and their opinion alone is of any real value. But unfortunately in literature, and especially in this Ionian literature, the normal person is the exception, and most of the writers we now have to consider seem to have been unmarried and childless.

The paucity of material, probably no great loss either in an artistic or a moral sense, has obscured the facts, but there seems little doubt that in this period literature was definitely used for the first time to degrade the position of women. The iambic metre was invented for the express purpose of satirical calumny, and the three chief iambic poets of the Alexandrian canon, Archilochus, Simonides, and Hipponax, in their scanty fragments all agree on one point: the chief object of their lampoons is —woman. At the beginning of this period the two sexes are fairly equal in their opportunities; at the end the female is plainly the inferior. Sappho and Erinna mark the turning-point in literature. Living at a time when it had not been made impossible for women to write, they showed that a woman could equal or surpass the male poets of her day. The few fragments of Erinna's verse that we possess, *e.g.*, the epigram on the portrait of Agatharchis and the pathetic elegy on the dead Baucis, reveal a talent at least as fine and strong as that of Alcæus; while of all the Greek lyrists, Sappho, both in reputation and as far as we can judge in actual achievement, holds by far the highest place.

Later ages, indeed, found it difficult to believe that Sappho was a woman at all. The scandal of male gossip was inspired by a genuine and pathetic belief that such a genius as hers must at least have been touched with masculine vices. But in Sappho's writings, which are our only real evidence, there is nothing distinctively 'mannish': she is neither gross nor tedious. In the technique of her art, metrical skill, the music of verse, she is at least the equal of any poet who has lived since her day; in thought and diction she is far superior to all her contemporaries.

In dealing with the Ionian poetry, exact dates are impossible, but the lyric age extends roughly from the middle of the seventh to the middle of the sixth century. The earliest writer in order of time, and in some ways the most important, is Archilochus, the Burns or Villon of Greece—outlaw, soldier of fortune, poet, the first man to introduce his own personal feelings into literature.

Archilochus has his own special reasons for hating women—'Archilochum proprio rabies armavit iambo'—and, as he says, he had learned the great lesson, 'If anyone hurts you, hurt her in return.' Betrothed to Cleobule, the daughter of a wealthy citizen of Paros, he found his marriage forbidden by the lady's father, Lycambes. The father's reasons may be guessed, even from the few fragments of Archilochus that still remain. But the poet turned abruptly from amorist to misogynist, and spent the rest of his life in railing against his lost mistress and womankind in general.

Both in love and war he is uncompromisingly frank. He tells us how he threw away his shield '*beside the bush in battle: but deuce take the shield, I will get another just as good, and at any rate I have escaped from death.*' His love poems are equally free-spoken. It is the actual image of his mistress that torments him when he cries, '*With myrtle boughs and roses fair she used to delight herself*'; and again, '*All her back and shoulders were covered by the shadow of her hair.*' But to his fierce spirit such love brings little comfort: '*Wretch that I am, like a dead man I lie, captive to desire, pierced with cruel anguish through all my bones*'; and, '*The longing that takes the strength from a man's limbs, it is that which overcomes me now.'*

Soon his love turns to hate and loathing, and he imputes to the woman the fault that is really his own: '*I was wronged, I have sinned. Aye! and many another man, methinks, will fall like me to ruin.*' His mistress now for him has lost her beauty. '*No longer does your soft flesh bloom fair; even as dry leaves it begins to wither.*' Like all women, she is false and full of guile: '*In one hand she carries water, in the other the fire of craft.*' To marry a woman now is, '*To take to one's house manifest ruin.*'

The folly of men and the falsity of women seem to have been the themes of the animal stories which Archilochus, like Æsop, composed. Woman is the fox; man is now the eagle, now the ape; but the fragments are too short for a certain judgment. What remains, indeed, of Archilochus is always tantalising in its incompleteness. Of his epigrams, for example, only three are left; here is a free translation of one of them: 'Miss High-and-mighty, as soon as she became a wedded wife, kicked her bonnet over the moon.'

Fortunately, however, we have preserved for us in Herodotus a much longer specimen of Archilochus' manner—a real Milesian tale, the story of Gyges and Candaules. The tale is handed down to us in Herodotus' prose, and it is impossible to disentangle the shares contributed by the Ionian poet and the Ionian historian; nor is it necessary; the story is typical of both.

Candaules makes the initial mistake of being enamoured of his own wife, and the second mistake of not believing Gyges when he is enlightened on the subject of female modesty. His folly naturally brings him to a bad end.

The story is interesting, but it is especially significant when we compare it with the tale of the same Gyges as told by Plato. There the sensual elements disappear, the interest centres in the magic ring, and the seduction of the queen and murder of the king form merely the hasty conclusion of the narrative. The difference between the two stories is the measure of the difference between the feminist philosopher and the libertine turned woman-hater.

But Archilochus at least has once loved a woman. Our next poet, Simonides of Amorgos, seems to have been a misogynist from birth. His work now only exists in fragments, but it is so significant of a frame of mind that the two longest passages that survive deserve a verbatim translation. The first runs thus:

Women, they are the greatest evil that God ever created. Even if they do appear to be useful at times, they usually turn out a curse to their owners. A man who lives with a wife never gets through a whole day without trouble, and it is no easy matter for him to drive away from his house that fiend abhorred, the foul fiend, Hunger. Moreover, just when a man is thinking to be merry at home—by God's grace or man's service —the woman always finds some ground of fault and puts on her armour for battle. Where there is a wife, you can never entertain a guest without fear of trouble. Again, the woman who seems to be most virtuous, mind you, may well be the most mischievous of all. Her husband gapes at her in admiration, but his neighbours laugh to see him, and the mistake he is making.

Every one will praise his own wife—men are shrewd enough for that—and then will talk scandal about his neighbour's, and all the time we do not realise that we are all in the same plight, for, as we said before, this is the greatest evil that God ever created.

The other fragment, the catalogue of women, is longer and better known. It begins:

From the first God made women's characters different. Into one kind of woman He put the mind of a pig, lank and bristly, and in her house everything lies about in disorder, bedraggled with mud and rolling on the floor, while she herself, unwashed, in dirty clothes sits in the mire and waxes fat.

The second woman God made out of a mischievous fox. She is cunning in all things alike; she knows everything, all that is bad and all that is good; often her speech is fair, but often it is evil, and her mood changes every day.

The third sort of woman was made out of a dog, and she is the true child of her mother, ever restless. She wants to hear and know about everything; she is always peering about and roaming around, growling even though there is no one in sight. A man cannot stop her with threats ; no, not even if in sudden anger he break her teeth with a stone. Soft talk is useless, too ; it is all the same even if she happen to be sitting among strangers : a man finds her a continual and hopeless nuisance.

The fourth woman the gods in heaven made out of mud—or rather they half made her—and then gave her to man. Such a one knows nothing, good or bad ; the only business she has sense enough for is eating. Even if God sends a bitter winter's day and she be shivering, she never will draw her chair closer to the fire.

The fifth woman was made out of the sea, and she has two minds within her. One day she is all smiles and gladness. A stranger seeing her in the house will praise her. 'In all the world,' says he, 'there is not a better or a fairer lady.' But another day she is insupportable to look at or to approach. She is filled with fury, like a bitch guarding her cubs : savage to all alike, friends and foes, detestable. Even so the sea often stands quiet and harmless, a joy to sailors in the summer tide, and often again is driven to madness by the thunderous waves. It is to the sea that such a woman is most like.

The sixth woman was made from an ass, grey of hide and stubborn against blows. Though you use reproaches and force, it is with difficulty you get her to give way to you and do her work satisfactorily. She is always eating, day and night ; she eats in her bedroom, she eats by the fireside. But if a man approaches to make love to her, she comes forward quickly enough to welcome him.

The seventh was made out of a polecat, a plaguy and a grievous kind. There is nothing fair or lovable in her, nothing pleasant, nothing charming, and any man who comes near she fills with nausea. She is a thief and annoys her neighbours, and often she gobbles up the sacrifice herself without offering any to the gods.

The eighth woman was the daughter of a mare, stepping daintily with flowing mane. She shudders at the thought of any servant's work or labour. She will never lay her hand to the millstone, nor lift up the sieve, nor throw the dung out of doors: she won't even sit near the kitchen stove, because she is afraid of the soot, and she makes her husband well acquainted with adversity. Every day, two or three times, she washes every speck of dirt off her, and anoints herself with unguents. Her hair is always luxuriant and well combed, with garlands of flowers upon it. Of course, such a woman is a fine sight for the men to see, but she is a curse to her owner, unless indeed he be a tyrant or sceptred king who has a fancy to pride himself on such delights.

The ninth woman came from a monkey: this sort is, indeed, pre-eminently the very greatest curse that God ever sent to men. Her features are shamefully ugly; such a woman, as she walks through a town, is a mockery to all men. She has a short neck, and moves with difficulty; she has no buttocks, her legs are all bone. Alas for the poor wretch who holds such an evil thing in his arms! But as for guile and tricks, she knows them all, and like a monkey she does not mind being laughed at. She never renders anyone a service, but all day long this is what she is seeking and looking for—how to do some one as much harm as she can.

The tenth woman was made out of a bee: happy the man who gets her! On her alone no breath of scandal lights, but she brings a life of happiness and prosperity. Husband and wife grow old together in love, and fair and glorious are her children. Famous among all women is she, and a grace divine encompasses her about. She takes no delight in sitting with other women when they are telling bawdy tales.

Such women as she are the best and wisest given by God to men : all the other kinds are a bane to men, and by God's decree a bane they always will be.

And so the fragment ends.

All this is pure misogyny ; but it is interesting to notice the especial faults which our poet imputes to womankind. They are chiefly the two vices which a surly master will always find in his servants, gluttony and idleness ; they work too little and eat too much. We are far removed in this world from our 'Feed the brute,' and it must be remembered that in a Greek household the work was hard, monotonous, and continual. There were no labour-saving appliances, for the hard work was chiefly done by women. Every mouthful of bread or porridge eaten in a Greek home had come into the house as a sack of dirty grain. First it was winnowed, and cleaned by hand ; then the grain was put into a small hand-mill, and by a laborious process of pestle and mortar it was ground into flour ; the flour was then made into dough, kneaded and baked ; every process being attended with the maximum of manual labour and general inconvenience, borne by the women of the house, while the master strolled about the city.

So also with the clothes and household fabrics :

every operation in their manufacture was done at home by the women. The master contented himself with buying the sheep-skins—and, as Theocritus lets us see, often did that very badly—which he then handed to his wife. First, the skins had to be washed and dried; then the wool was cut off and carded; then by a laborious process of spinning the wool was turned into yarn, and finally on a hand-loom the yarn was woven into cloth: the same piece of stuff, so excellent was the workmanship, often serving for coat, blanket and shroud.

It is obvious, then, that an idle wife—if such a thing existed—or a wife who ate more than her share of the laboriously prepared bread, would be a great grief to her lord and master, who was himself too busy with the higher work of politics to attend to such things, and that the machinery of the household would be put very much out of gear. It may well be that Simonides was unfortunate in his choice of a helpmate, for as Hipponax, the third of this company, mournfully complains, '*It is hard to get a wife who will both bring you a good dowry and then do all the work.*' Hipponax, if we may judge him by some forty short fragments, was a thoroughly disagreeable person; he is always asking and being refused; he varies complaints with abuse or downright threats. '*Hold my coat,*' he cries, '*and I will knock out his eye. I've got two right hands, and I never miss when I throw.'* On the subject of women he does not say so much as the other two, for the range of his thought is almost confined to carnal delights. A fair sample of his style is this fragment : '*There are only two days in your life that your wife gives you pleasure: the day you marry her and the day you bury her.*'

This insistence on the physical side of love runs through all the elegiac and lyric poetry of the age. Love to Mimnermus is a thing of secret kisses, of chambering and wantonness, and it depends alone on physical attractions. A young man is happy, for he is handsome and desirable; an old man is wretched, to women an object of scorn. The satiety that comes from excess of sensual pleasure is the main cause of the melancholy pessimism that broods over much of Ionian literature. Of Alcæus and his Lycus, Anacreon and his Bathyllus, Theognis and Cyrnus, it is unnecessary now to speak, but it is difficult to believe such amiable apologists as Mr. Benecke when they try to show that a fine idealism was the inspiration of these relationships. Neither the character of the men's writings nor that of their time and country give much ground for such confidence, and if we seek the purity of love's passion we must turn to Sappho.

Among all the foulness of her time Sappho shines out like a star. No loss in literature is so lamentable as the loss of the nine books of her poems that the

Alexandrian library possessed ; no treasure in literature is quite so precious as the fragments that various chances have preserved for us. And, luckily, the number of those fragments is still increasing, as will be seen by a comparison of the two best studies of Sappho in recent years, the exquisite collection of translations issued by Mr. Wharton in 1886, and the brilliant monograph on the new fragments by Mr. J. M. Edmonds in 1912. Even since that date fresh poems have come to light, and we do not know what Egypt may have yet in store.

In all the fragments, new or old, there is an indefinable quality of personal feeling. Sappho, it has been said, has left us only a fragment of her work, but it is a fragment of her soul. Her friend and rival, Alcæus, is a great poet, but he lacks the fiery intensity of her inspiration, which gives life even to the briefest phrase that some grammarian has quoted for a rare word. Take the lines that Rossetti adapted :

Like the sweet apple which reddens upon topmost bough,
A-top on the topmost twig—which the pluckers forget somehow,
Forget it not—nay, but got it not, for none could get it till now.
Like the wild hyacinth flower, which on the hills is found,
Which the passing feet of the shepherds for ever tear and wound,
Until the purple blossom is trodden into the ground.

Or, again, this other :

Dead, dead.—In death,
Below the ground, bereft of breath,
Silent, alone, the close-shut tomb enfoldeth thee.
To my songs thou wouldst not hearken, and songless
  shalt thou be ;
Thou wouldst not love me here on earth,
In death thou shalt loveless be.

Mr. Edmonds, in his translations, has kept much of the simple charm of the Greek :

I have a little daughter rare,
That's like the golden flowers fair,
My Cleis.
I would not take all Lydia wide,
No, nor lovely Greece beside,
For Cleis.

And this, a portion of a new fragment :

And often as her way she wanders,
And on gentle Attis ponders,
With sad longing love opprest,
Her heart devours her tender breast
  Till she cries, in pain,
' Oh, come to me,' for you and I
Know the burden of her cry,
Since Night, which hath the myriad ears,
Sends her word of what she hears
  Across the severing main.

This tender simplicity is the soul of Sappho, and in her verse even a few words will suggest a picture :

Come to me, O Love :
O Love, the inheritor, enter in.

Everywhere is swept and garnished,
Everything is prepared.
The fire of my heart burns brightly,
All my body is food for thee,
And on my bosom thou shalt sleep the long night through.

ἐπὶ δὲ στήθεος ἐννυχεύσεις. Surely no one save Sappho has touched so closely the heart of love and poetry.

IV.—The Milesian Tales

The chief characteristic of Ionian literature is a certain softness, a kind of laxity of morals corresponding to a looseness of political organisation. The Ionian man was a convinced believer in freedom —for himself; but he was by no means a believer in the discipline which alone makes freedom possible. Both in sexual matters and in politics, his desire for freedom and his desire for pleasure were constantly at cross-purposes. He wished to be independent of women; but he was not meant by nature to be a monk, and he purchased his apparent freedom by yielding to a sensuality far more degrading than that of women's love. He wished to be independent of Persia; but he was not a born soldier, and he finally bought a pretence of autonomy by the payment of tribute to a Persian satrap, forfeiting his manhood for the sake of peace.

The Ionians were, indeed, a strange medley of qualities, and with them intellectual activity stood in sharp contrast with moral and physical sloth. They were essentially a race of city dwellers; for them the charm of the country and of nature had little attraction, and their civilisation found its most perfect expression during the seventh and sixth centuries in the splendid luxury of such towns as the Ionian Miletus, in Asia Minor, and the Achæan Sybaris, in South Italy. The two cities were closely connected by ties of trade and social intercourse, and in both places material prosperity led quickly to moral corruption, and voluptuousness became the rule of life. Like Buenos Ayres to-day, Miletus and Sybaris were trading ports founded in a new country, and the rapid growth of riches discouraged the manlier virtues. The mixture of races was a danger, the climate favoured voluptuous pleasures, and the bracing stimulus of war was, until too late, absent. The moral and sexual degradation that resulted from this unbridled pursuit of pleasure found its expression, as we have seen, in literature. The tale of Ganymede, the episode of the tricked husband in the *Iliad*, and the catalogue of women in Simonides, are fair samples of Ionian thought. No one of the three has any moral value ; indeed, a strict Puritan would probably refuse to let them soil his lips ; but they are at least decent enough to be written down in a literary form, and to pass muster, if they are not too closely examined.

There was, however, another and even less creditable class of story of which literary historians tell us little, but which, probably, was first invented in such towns as Miletus and Sybaris in the seventh and sixth centuries, during the time of their greatest prosperity—the so-called Milesian Tales. Usually circulating by word of mouth, they endured for centuries, and occasionally make a furtive appearance in history, but their significance in sexual morality has not always been appreciated. In dealing with them as literature we are confronted with a threefold difficulty: firstly, many of the most typical specimens of this style were never written down at all; secondly, most of the stories that found a footing in literature were blotted out by the righteous indignation of Christian moralists; thirdly, in the case of the few that do survive, it is neither possible nor desirable to introduce them to a modern audience. But, though they are the least estimable part of our inheritance from ancient literature, their influence on ancient morals was very great, and their tendency was so definitely to ruin any reasonable conception of sex relationships that they force themselves into notice.

Though sometimes written in prose, their natural medium was the iambic measure, invented by Archilochus, and they were meant both for a male and female audience. Iambus the jester, *Pierrot*, has his female counterpart in Iambë, *Pierrette*, who appears in the Homeric hymn to Demeter, and by her capers forces the sad goddess to smile once more. This is, perhaps, the one justification of the tales; in their more innocent form they were intended to purge away that feeling of melancholy of which, as the precursor of madness, the Greeks were so much afraid, by exciting the emotion of laughter; just as tragedy effects the same purpose by exciting the emotions of pity and fear. But this sort of humour in Athens and Ionia soon degenerated into coarseness, and Iambe, her name now changed to Baubo, as we see her in the ritual statuette, a woman sitting on a pig, played a prominent and a shameful part in the Eleusinian mysteries of Demeter. The worship of the sorrowing mother—Mater Dolorosa—was made the cloak for nameless obscenities, and the influence of religion was added to that of literature to degrade men's conception of women. These were the sort of verses and images to which Aristotle alludes in the Seventh Book of the *Politics*; and this is one of the reasons for Plato's objection to poetry; better no literature at all, he thinks, than literature degraded to these ends.

The worst type of Milesian or Sybaritic tale was definitely meant to stimulate the animal passions, and owed little to any qualities of humour or imagination. The sense of artistic fitness which the Athenians always possessed kept this kind of stories out of written literature during the great period, and confined them to the gossip of the perfumers' and barbers' shops. But as soon as the decadence began, these 'Ionian poems,' as Athenæus calls them, became a recognised branch of letters, and we hear of their chief practitioners, writers of 'facetiæ,' the 'Hilarodoi,' the 'Simodoi,' and the 'Lysiodoi.'

Among the more notorious authors were Simus the Magnesian, Alexander the Ætolian, Pyres the Milesian, and Sotades of Maronea, who gives his name to that whole class of licentious writings which is represented in modern times by the sotadic satire of Nicholas Chorier. Sotades, however, did not confine himself to the comparatively safe pastime of libelling women. He ventured to write lampoons upon Ptolemy Philadelphus and his sister Arsinoe, was caught on the island where he had taken refuge, put into a jar with a leaden top, and drowned.

But the most famous, or infamous, of all the class is Aristides, usually called, but on very little evidence, 'of Miletus,' who lived perhaps in the second century before Christ. Of the man and his book we have little direct knowledge, but he was translated into Latin by Sisenna, the companion of Sulla in his voluptuous debauchery, and copies of this version were found by the Parthians in the tents of the Roman officers after the battle of Carrhæ. Even the Parthians, as Plutarch tells us, were disgusted by Aristides, and Ovid tries to use him as a shelter for himself against the charge of immoral writing. The Roman poet who, though a libertine, was at least free from some of the grosser vices of his age, complains bitterly in his exile of the difference in treatment meted out to Aristides and himself. '*Aristides was not banished,*' he cries, '*and yet he fathered all the scandalous stories of Miletus: the authors amongst us who now put together Sybaritic stories go unpunished.*'

Sybaritic and Milesian were the descriptive adjectives used even in Ovid's time for this kind of writing, and we can trace its popularity and influence in Rome. Quotations are obviously impossible, and indeed the *genre* does not depend on literary grace. One author alone, Petronius, possesses sufficient skill to make it tolerable, and the viler portions of the 'Satyricon' are the most real examples of the literature that was inspired by Miletus, and by Milesian ideas of womankind. The natural coarseness of the Roman mind gave this sort of story a greater prominence than the Greeks ever allowed, but it will probably be correct to trace its first origin to the coast of Ionia in the seventh century and especially to the metropolis of the Ionian States.

From the beginning at Miletus the relations between men and women were notoriously bad, and, as Herodotus tells us, they had some historical justification. 'The first settlers at Miletus,' he says, 'having no wives of their own, killed the men and seized the women of the country.' On account of this massacre, the women established the law and imposed upon themselves an oath, which they handed down to their daughters, to this effect:

> They should never eat at the same table with their husbands, nor should any woman ever call her husband by his name. For they had killed their fathers, their husbands, and their sons, and after so doing had forced them to become their wives.

This is the first incident in the history of Miletus, an episode not unlike the story of the Lemnian women, and it explains a great deal. In the chief city of Ionia, enmity, not love, was the law between husband and wife. Domestic life was poisoned, and literature caught the infection. By action and reaction the mischief spread, and it is impossible for us now fully to estimate its extent. But we cannot doubt the effect that Ionian literature had in lowering men's estimate of women, and thereby degrading all their ideals of social life. The three great curses of Greek civilisation—sexual perversion, infanticide, and the harem system—all come into prominence during the sixth century, and there is good reason to believe that it was just at this time that the natural increase of population was checked, and the slow process of race suicide begun. If Ionia was the cradle of Greek culture, as we know it, from Ionia also came the germs of that moral disease which made a fatal counterpoise to the intellectual supremacy of Greece.

In the worse type of Milesian Tale immorality takes its most revolting form; but there was another and more pleasing form of story, also invented in Ionia about this time, which occasionally is called by the same title, and is best known to us in the collection of Æsop's Fables. Æsop himself, the lame slave who was made by tradition the fellow-servant of the fair courtesan, Rhodopis, and so a contemporary of Sappho, is hardly more a real person than Homer, and his name was used as a convenient shelter for two slightly different kinds of humorous story. There were the well-known animal fables which are common to the whole Mediterranean and Asiatic world, and in Æsop find a Greek dress, and beside them a sort of humorous anecdote, sometimes trivial, sometimes coarse, but always strongly realistic.

They were especially popular at Athens. 'Tell them a funny tale of Æsop, or of Sybaris,' says the old gentleman in Aristophanes' 'Wasps,' 'something you heard at the club'; and later on in the play, when Bdelycleon is intoxicated, we get two specimens of the style. Like our Limericks, they are in verse, with a catch refrain: '*A woman at Sybaris once,*' and '*Æsop one day,*' and although they are not particularly humorous, it must be remembered that they are the witticisms of a drunken man. The first runs thus :

> Æsop one night was going back from dinner, when a bitch began to bark at him, a bold, drunken creature. Thereupon said he : 'Dear, dear ! my good bitch, if you were to sell that foul tongue of yours and buy some flour, you would be more sensible.'

The other is this :

> A woman of Sybaris once broke a jug. The jug got a friend to act as witness, and laid a claim for damages. Thereupon the lady said : 'By the virgin, if you would but let the lawyers alone and buy some sticking-plaster you would show more wisdom.'

The fables of Æsop are now a nursery classic, for, like the *Arabian Nights* and *Gulliver's Travels*, they have been turned by the kindly irony of time to a use which their authors hardly contemplated. But in their Milesian shape there was always an underlying vein of satire, even in the animal stories. The male animals, the eagle and the lion, are brave and generous ; the females, the fox and the weasel, are cunning and treacherous.

Moreover, as we see in the Greek version of Babrius and the Latin of Phædrus, separated though they be from the original by a gap of centuries, there was a great deal of matter in the Æsopian stories which was plainly misogynistic.

As examples, we may take from Babrius, Fable 10 :

A man fell in love with an ugly, dirty slave-girl, his own property, and readily gave her all she asked. She had her fill of gold: fine purple robes trailing at her ankles, and soon she began to rival the mistress of the house. 'The goddess of love,' thought she, 'is the cause of all this,' and she honoured her with votive tapers, going every day to sacrifice and prayer with supplications and requests. But at last the goddess came in a dream while they were asleep, and appearing to the slave-girl, she said, 'Do not thank me, or suppose that I have made you beautiful: I am angry with that fellow there, and so he thinks you fair.'

Belief in women's beauty, we see, is mere infatuation, and so is belief in their truth, as No. 16 shows :

A country nurse once threatened a whining child: 'Stop, or I will throw you to the wolf.' The wolf heard the words, and supposing that the old dame was speaking the truth, waited patiently for the meal which he thought would soon be ready. It was not till evening that the child fell asleep, and the wolf, who had been waiting on slow hope, went off home very hungry, his mouth really agape. 'How is it you have come home empty-handed?' said his wife, who had been keeping house. 'It's very unusual.' But the wolf replied: 'What would you have? I have trusted a woman.'

No. 32 is a curious reminiscence of Simonides :

Once upon a time a cat fell in love with a comely man, and glorious Cypris, the mother of Desire, allowed her to change her shape and take a woman's body, one so fair that all men desired her. The young man saw her, fell captive in his turn and arranged to wed. The marriage feast was just prepared when a mouse ran by, and the bride, jumping down from the high couch, rushed after it. So the banquet came to an end, and Love, who had had a merry jest, departed too—for even he could not fight against nature.

No. 22 is more outspoken :

Once upon a time a middle-aged man—not young, but not yet old, his hair a mixture of black and white—feeling that he still had leisure for love and merriment, took two mistresses, one young, one old. Now the young woman wanted to see in her lover a young man, the old dame desired some one as old as herself. So, every time, the girl plucked out any hairs that she could find turning white, while the old lady did the same to the black hairs, until young and old together at last pulled out all the hair he had and left him bald. *Moral :* Pitiable is the man who falls into the hands of women : they bite and bite until they strip him to the bone.

So in the fable of the lion who falls in love with a maiden, the noble animal strips himself of claws and teeth, and everything that makes him formidable, to please the girl, and for his reward is beaten to death.

In all these stories there is a note of satirical depreciation, but the best example of the cynical humour which inspires the whole class is to be found in the tale of the Ephesian Widow. Phædrus gives a brief version ; in Petronius the story is put into the mouth of the satyr-poet Eumolpus, and in a condensed form it will perhaps bear quotation. 'There was once a matron of Ephesus so notoriously virtuous that all the women of the neighbouring towns used to come and gaze upon her as at a wonderful spectacle.' So it begins, and the first sentence, which might come from Voltaire's *Candide*, gives the spirit in which it is written. The lady's husband died, and not satisfied with the ordinary signs of grief, the bereaved wife insisted on following the corpse to the underground chamber where it was laid. There the lady 'with singular and exemplary constancy,' remained with it for five days, deaf to the entreaties of relatives and magistrates, refusing all food, and attended only by one servant-girl whose business it was to share her mistress' grief and renew the taper which alone lit up the sepulchral chamber.

'The whole country was full of the story,' so the tale runs, 'and men of every class agreed that this was a real and brilliant example of virtue and affection in a woman—*the only one they had ever known.*'

In the meantime, however, some robbers had been crucified near the place, and a soldier on guard over the crosses noticed the light of the taper gleaming in the darkness. Yielding to the weakness of human nature, he made his way down to the vault, and was surprised to find a pretty woman, where he had expected to see a ghost. But he soon realised the situation—that the lady could not get over the loss of her man—and so he brought his traps down to the cellar and began to address some words of comfort to her. 'Do not persist in useless grief,' said he, 'do not rend your breast with unavailing sobs; all of us will come to this; we all have but one final resting-place.' His attempt at consolation—which, though well-meant, is certainly somewhat commonplace—only irritated the lady, and he turned his attention to the servant (for in this sort of stories there is always a soubrette) and induced her to partake of his rations.

The girl was then able to persuade her mistress to follow her example, and soon all three were eating and drinking together.

'You know,' so says Eumolpus, 'the result of a good meal: the soldier was soon as successful in overcoming the matron's resolute virtue as he had been in overcoming her resolute desire for death.'

The doors of the vault were closed, so that it might appear that the good lady had breathed her last over her husband's body; the soldier brought down all sorts of comestibles, and two or three days and nights were spent in dalliance.

Meanwhile the crucified robbers were quite forgotten, and on the third morning the soldier found that one of the crosses was empty, for the body had been removed for burial by the relatives in the night. He explained his plight to the lady, and announced his intention of committing suicide, the proper penalty, as he said, for his neglect of duty.

But the matron was as compassionate as she was virtuous, and 'Heaven forfend!' she cried. 'I cannot bear to see two such dear men both depart from life. I would rather pay over the dead than lose the living.' So she told the soldier to take the husband's body out of its receptacle and fix it on the vacant cross. 'The soldier gladly followed the clever lady's ingenious idea, and the next day people were wondering how it was that a dead man had found his way to the cross.'

The Ephesian Widow represents the Milesian Tales at their best; at their worst they are only to be read by those who can touch pitch and not be defiled. In themselves they are beneath contempt, but they have a very considerable importance in the history of the world, and especially in the history of the relations of the sexes. The perverse ideas that underlie them were transplanted from Ionia to Athens, and, recommended by the literary genius o Athenian writers, they have had an influence on later thought which the Ionian pornographers would never have secured.

V.—Athens in the Fifth Century

We have traced the main tendencies of Ionian thought, and have seen how the degradation of women involved a corresponding degradation of literature. Its very offensiveness protects a great deal of Ionian work from notice, but it has been necessary to quote some of the less noisome specimens, for it must be remembered that this immorality of literature was both the cause and the result of the low opinion in which women were held. The motives which inspired the whole school of writers were utterly contemptible, the means they employed were not much better; but they were successful in their purpose. When Athens took over the leadership of Greece, she took over from Ionia the idea of women as inferior creatures, and during all the great period of Athenian history women were a subject class. It became no longer necessary to slander them; they were simply neglected.

A woman's life at Athens in the fifth century B.C. was a dreary business. She was confined closely to the house, a harem prisoner, but without any of that luxurious ease which the harem system has sometimes offered as a solace for the loss of freedom. An Athenian house was small, dark, and uncomfortable, and a woman's day was occupied with a long round of monotonous work. Occasionally she was allowed out of prison to walk in some sacred procession, as we see the quiet line of girls marshalled on the Parthenon frieze, but all the amusements of the town were closed against her. From the school and the gymnasium, from the Odeon and the Academy, from public meetings and from private banquets, women were jealously debarred. It is doubtful whether they were permitted even to enter the theatre of Dionysus ; and their shopping quarter, where they bought their rouge and white lead, was in the most remote and inaccessible part of the city.

The whole structure of social life was arranged to suit men and to exclude women. It is true that the patron divinity of the state was a woman, Athena, but the goddess was divested of feminine attributes. She became the ideal Athens, a conception as far remote from an anthropomorphic divinity as any race has ever possessed.

The stages by which women were reduced to this condition of inferiority are, in the general obscurity of early Athenian history, quite unknown ; but there can be little doubt that the whole position was due to Ionian influence. The legal status of women, especially in relation to property, seems to have been changed by definite enactment about the end of the sixth century B.C., and in the *Suppliant Maidens* of Æschylus there are traces of the conflict of principles on which the change was based. Henceforward, in the eyes of the Athenian law, a woman was merely an appanage of any property which she chanced to inherit, and her nearest male relative had to take charge of her person—a *damnosa hereditas* for which the material advantages of her estate served as compensation.

Moreover, women in Athens were married far too young, for the average age was about fifteen, and the result of these early marriages was that by the time a woman had arrived at years of discretion and might have been an intellectual companion for her husband, her beauty too often was gone and she herself was worn out, a premature old woman. For girls no education was considered necessary, and throughout their childhood they were kept in constant seclusion. They were regarded only as potential bearers of children, and the most extreme precautions known to modern eugenics were apparently practised before marriage. But even as mothers they were not very efficient, for their physique suffered from the narrowness of their lives, and the wet-nurse—Titthe—was to be found in most families. Just as the Breton and Norman girls migrate to Paris, so those Athenian households that could afford the expense would hire the robust women of Sparta to take the mother's place. Alcibiades, for example, was suckled by a Lacedæmonian nurse, and was not altogether an alien when, exiled from Athens, he took refuge in the Peloponnese. It was not in Athens, but at Sparta, or in the islands where girls wrestled and raced with young men, that Paionios found the model for his 'Victory,' with her flying feet, deep bosom, and firm, rounded limbs; and in Aristophanes, when Lysistrata assembles the women of Greece, the Athenians can scarcely refrain their half-envious admiration of the buxom vigour of the Spartan Lampeto.

At Athens the restriction of women to one function meant that even that one function was badly performed, and all through the great period the Athenian race was slowly declining in numbers.

In one respect alone was there little difference between the sexes at Athens—that of dress. There was no distinction of sex, as there was no distinction of rank. In an Attic tragedy a chorus of generals, of fishermen, and of flower-girls would all appear in much the same garb. In Asia both sexes wore trousers (θύλακοι, 'bags'), which the Greeks regarded with amused contempt. In Athens neither sex did. There were some slight varieties in shape, material, and colour, but, speaking generally, it is correct to say that an Athenian lady—or an Athenian gentleman was dressed informally when she or he had one blanket draped about their person. Full dress consisted of another blanket over the first, and the art of dress consisted in suitable pinning and the proper arrangement of the folds.

But when a woman left her husband's house and went abroad, she had to don the symbol of her slavery, the 'kredemnon.' This article was a kind of yashmak-veil, drawn across the face to protect a woman from the gaze of strange men, not her lawful owners. It gave its wearer the white cheeks of the odalisque, and shut her off from the freedom of the outside world. It was, like our cap and apron, the badge of servitude, and to escape from it the only way was to become a slave indeed, for the slave-woman alone could walk abroad with open face.

This is what Euripides means when he makes the captive Andromache sob: 'And I, even I, was dragged from my royal bower down to the sea-beach with nothing about my head save hideous slavery.' (*And.* 109.)

And so Hecuba, in the *Trojan Women*, a slave bare-footed and bare-headed, crouches on the ground to escape from the gaze of men, and cries: 'Guide me to my bed of straw and to the stones which now will hide my face.' (*Trojan Women*, 508.) Slavery in ancient times was a hard fate, but for many an

Athenian woman it could have had but little terror. A wife was already the property of her husband, and slaves and women are commonly classed together.

The Athenian, however, with all his faults was a genuine lover of freedom, and did not care for slaves. Neither his wife nor the flute-girls, whose charms could be bought by any bidder, could really satisfy him, strange mixture that he was of sensuality and intellect. The only women whose company he desired were those called, half in jest, half in earnest, the Hetairai, ' the close companions,' the same word being used for those political associations which formed the closest link between man and man.

The Hetairai were foreign women, and stood outside the law : they were not Athenian citizens, and so had no privileges ; but, on the other hand, they were not under restraint. Often highly educated, it was their business to take part in all men's interests : they were their own mistresses, engaged freely in the political life of Athens, and in many cases exercised very great influence even in affairs of state. To their personal attractions they added social charm and a long training in the arts of pleasure, and the contrast between them and the Athenian wives may be illustrated if we compare the life of an actress of the *Comédie Française* with that of an inmate of a Turkish harem. The French actress and the Japanese geisha are the nearest modern parallels to the Greek hetaira, and all three owe their existence as a class to much the same social conditions, a high standard of culture and intelligence, a low standard of sexual morality.

Such were the conditions of Athenian life, and we shall find them reflected in literature. The great lyric poets, Simonides, Pindar, Bacchylides, concern themselves almost exclusively with men; Æschylus alone, in this, as in most things, the exact antithesis of the typical Athenian, regards women as creatures possessed of mind and soul. In sharp contrast to the tragedian is Herodotus, and a comparison between their views is possible, for, although the historian is a considerably younger man, a good deal of his material goes back to an earlier date, and in social matters especially he often represents the ideas of the first years of the fifth century.

Herodotus, great traveller and charming personality though he is, is still a true Ionian. There is frequently a Milesian flavour about his tales—for instance the story of Rhampsinitus and the robber—and it is not unfair to say that in his researches into ancient tribal life and folklore he is especially interested in such savage customs as put women in an inferior place. The account of the native races of Libya in the last chapters of the fourth book of the History will afford an example.

But the grandeur of his main theme, the struggle between Athens and Persia, raised the historian from these doubtful interests, and in the last five books of his work there is little depreciation of women as a class. It is true that women scarcely come into the narrative, and that Xerxes' remark about Artemisia, ' My men have become women and my women have become men,' is framed to suit the ideas of an Athenian, as it would have suited the Romans, who could hardly conceive of a Queen. It is scarcely as appropriate in the mouth of a Persian whose own mother, Atossa, was then acting as regent. But this is a small point and, speaking generally, there is little in the last part of the History to offend.

Herodotus is really animated by an ardent patriotism and a genuine love of liberty. ' Isonomy,' he says—and many English race-goers will agree with him—' the very sound of the word is most excellent.' But it must be remembered that his patriotism is for males only, and that his equality before the law is an equality from which women were shut out; for even Plato makes isonomy between men and women the last and almost incredible stage of democratic licence.

So it is in the earlier books alone that the baser manner is evident, and one example of it will suffice to give a proof of the difference between the Ionian spirit which brought about the enslavement of women and the spirit of enlightenment which rebelled against that servitude.

We will take the story of Io, as told by Æschylus and Herodotus, for the ancient legends of Greece, subjects alike for history and drama, have one great advantage: their main outlines were impersonal and known to all; details, treatment, and interpretation could be varied to express the artist's personal thought. Io, the daughter of Inachus, king of Argos, was beloved by Zeus: through the jealousy of Hera she was changed into a cow, and after long wanderings regained her mortal shape and found rest in Egypt, where she became mother of Epaphus, first king of the land. Such is the legend, and this is Herodotus' version of it:

The Persians say that some Phœnicians once brought a cargo of merchandise to Argos. The women of the town, among them Io, came down to the seashore to bargain. The Phœnicians seized the women and carried them off to Egypt. Now to carry off women by violence the Persians think is the act of a wicked man; to trouble about avenging them is the act of a fool; to pay no regard to them when carried off is the part of a wise man; for it is clear that, if they had not wished it themselves, they would not be ravished. Such is the Persian account, but as regards Io the Phœnicians do not agree. They say that they used no violence in taking her to Egypt, but that she had an intrigue with their captain when he was at Argos. When she discovered that she was likely to become a mother she was afraid of her parents, and to hide her secret came of her own accord with them to Egypt.'

All the poetry and romance of the story have disappeared: realism has triumphed. Io is a woman; on the best interpretation of her conduct she is vain and imprudent; she shows herself to strange men, and is carried off by them, although, as the story is at pains, though not very logically, to add, it must have been with her own consent. On the worst interpretation she is a mere wanton. She allows a sea-captain to seduce her, and then deserts her home, her parents, and her native land.

Listen now to Æschylus—in the beautiful version by Mr. E. R. Bevan:

> The chambers, where I housed, a virgin hidden,
> Strange faces aye in the night would visit, wooing
> With sooth suggestion: 'Oh, most huge in fortune,
> Most happiest of all maidens—wherefore maiden,
> Oh, wherefore so long maiden, when there waits thee
> Wedlock the highest? He, the Lord of Heaven,
> Is waxen hot, pierced with desire of thee,
> Yea, and with thee would tread the passages
> Of love's delight. Now therefore foot not from thee,
> O child, the bed of the Highest; but do this,
> Go forth to where the meadow is deep, the field
> Of Lerna—stations of the household flock,
> Home of thy father's herds—go even thither,
> That so the eye of Zeus may ease desire.'
>
> With such-like dreams the kingly dark for me
> Was ever fraught, me miserable: till, ridden,

> I gat me heart to open to my father
> The visions and the dreams of night. And he
> To Pytho, yea, and even to Dodona,
> Sent embassage on embassage, inquiring
> What thing he had need to do, or what word speak,
> To pleasure them that rule us. And they came,
> Bringing still back burden of wavering lips,
> Sentences, blind, dark syllables. At last
> A word clear-visaged came to Machus
> Enjoining plainly and saying he should thrust me
> Forth of the house, forth of the land, to wander
> At large, a separate thing even to the last
> Confines of earth.

The story is the same, but the treatment is different, and the two passages illustrate the difference between romantic idealism and realistic depreciation.

But Io, in the *Prometheus*, is only one of the gallery of Æschylus' heroines, for in his art women take the foremost place. The dramatist is at variance with his age, and his fervent patriotism is almost the sole bond of union between him and his fellows. Æschylus is a mystic ; he believed in the Delphic inspiration, and took an interest in religious speculation. His contemporaries were materialists, suspected the politics of Delphi, and regarded religion simply as a ceremony Æschylus was a conservative in politics, although a liberal in thought ; Athens was already becoming an extreme democracy. Finally, Æschylus bases his theatre on women, and makes them the chief agents of the drama, while the ordinary woman of his time was shut out altogether from the active business of life.

But he is an unconscious feminist, and the definite purpose which we find in Euripides is quite absent from his plays. It shows, however, a strange lack of appreciation to reproach him, as some critics have done, with neglecting the feminine interest. Of the seven tragedies that the Byzantine tradition has preserved for us, four, if their subject was handled by a modern dramatist, would be called feminist problem plays, and in the other three the female characters supply most of the dramatic interest, even though the first idea of the plot might seem to put them in the second plan of action.

Of the lost plays, many, as far as we may judge by their titles and meagre fragments, have the same characteristic. The most famous, the *Niobe*, had for its central figure the sorrowing mother, such another as Euripides' Hecuba in the first scene of the *Trojan Women*, and represented perhaps in much the same fashion, for Æschylus, like most Athenian women, knew full well the dramatic value of silence, and the pathos of Niobe's situation needs no long speeches. So, if we possessed the *Callisto*, the legend of the maiden changed into a bear, the *Penelope*, the *Iphigenia*, or the *Oreithyia*, that favourite Athenian story of the young girl roaming on the sea-shore and carried off by the fierce god to his northern fastness, we should appreciate even more vividly than we can now the romantic side of the tragedian's art. It is a significant fact in this connection that of the sixty odd titles of lost plays which have come down to us, nearly half are names of women. Moreover, in seventeen of these plays, the title is taken from the chorus, and in the Æschylean Theatre the chorus is generally the central figure in the dramatic action. Such titles as the 'Daughters of the Sun,' the 'Nurses of Dionysus,' the 'Daughters of Nereus,' and the 'Bacchanal Women,' suggest at any rate romantic plays with a strong feminine interest; such others as the 'Women of the Bedchamber,' the 'Water-carriers,' and the 'Women of Etna,' might well be examples of that realistic treatment of women's life of which we have an example in the Nurse of the 'Libation-bearers.' Arguments drawn merely from the names of lost plays are obviously of little value, except in so far as they strengthen the definite evidence which the existing tragedies supply, but an examination of the remaining seven plays will show that the first and greatest of Athenian dramatists was deeply impressed with the potentialities for good and evil of the female mind.

VI.—Æschylus and Sophocles

Of the seven plays of Æschylus that remain, three—the *Seven against Thebes*, the *Persians*, and the *Prometheus*—are concerned with battles, and with strife among men and among gods. It might be expected that women here would play but a small part, but, as a matter of fact, in two of the three the chorus, the intermediary between poet and audience, is composed of women, and in the third a woman is the chief character.

The *Seven against Thebes* is a patriotic drama, 'crammed full of the spirit of war,' as the poet himself describes it, and also full of speeches. The male characters talk; what little action there is in the play falls to the women of the chorus. Their first song, for example, when they call on the gods to save them from the ravages of war, was probably accompanied by more vigorous movements than anything in the rest of the tragedy. The unsympathetic male, Eteocles, addresses them, it is true, as 'unbearable creatures' and 'detestable animals,' and says, 'For my own part, I never want to share my house with any womankind, nor take them to my troubles and my joys;' but his remarks are strictly in keeping with his unpleasant character, and the poet instinctively relies on the female characters for his chief dramatic interest. So in the *Persians*, a chronicle play composed mainly of choral odes and messengers' speeches, the queen-mother, Atossa, takes the first place in the action, and the psychological contrast lies between her womanly strength and Xerxes' manly weakness. In the *Prometheus*, certainly, most of the characters—gods and demi-gods—are males, but they have little dramatic significance. As far as they are concerned, the play is a good example of what Maeterlinck calls the 'static drama.' The characters stand still, *and talk.* The action is in the hands of the female characters, the pathetic figure of the wandering cow-maiden, Io, and the contrasted group of the mermaid chorus, the daughters of the sea. These latter are perhaps the most charming of all the poet's creations, and the fragrance that heralds their approach, when, casting away modesty, they venture to appear before a man, spreads through the whole play. Sympathising, but not quite without merriment; inquisitive, but staunch in the hour of danger; they are just such characters as Nausicaa herself.

In these three plays, then, the feminine interest has forced its way, as it were, into the plot, which in its first form offered women no place. The *Seven against Thebes*, a ' fragment from the table of Homer,' differs chiefly from the epic in the feminine element that has been imported by the chorus ; the *Persians*, dealing with the same events as those described by Herodotus, has for its point of difference the prominence given to the female character, Atossa ; the *Prometheus*, which tells the story of the conflict between the fierce young god and the philanthropic old demiurge, relies for its dramatic interest largely on the episodes of the Nereides and Io ; episodes which, strictly speaking, have nothing to do with the main plot.

This feminism, inherent in the poet's mind, finds full expression in the remaining four plays. The *Suppliant Women*, for example, archaic though it seems to us, deals with a social problem and a question of law, which was hotly debated in the poet's time, and finally, in spite of his advocacy, settled against the women. The question is this—' Should a woman be compelled to marry a man she dislikes, and to hand over to him the control of her property, merely because he is the nearest male relative ? ' Æschylus answers in the negative ; Athenian law *decided in the affirmative.*

The characters in the play are nearly all women, the fifty daughters of Danaus, accompanied by their old father, who have fled from Egypt to Greece in order to escape from the violence of their cousins, the sons of Ægyptus, who wish to marry them by force. It is a lyric drama, and the burden of the action and the music rests with the women. The agony of the crowd of girls crouching helpless at the altar is depicted in the most entrancing melody; they are not regarded as separate individuals, but as representing women in general; their plight is that of all womankind, and the problem is presented as universal. Swarthy daughters of the South, they call upon their god to help them, the god who once found delight in the arms of their ancestress, Io; and in the play their prayer is answered. The King of Argos protects and gives them shelter, the Egyptian herald who would have taken them back is scornfully dismissed. Of the three male characters Danaus is the most interesting, and his advice to his daughters is applicable to women generally in ancient times:

> Children, you must be prudent: let your utterance be attended before all by absence of boldness: a modest face and a tranquil eye: no wanton looks. Be not forward in your speech nor prolix: people here are very prone to take offence. And remember to be submissive—you are needy foreign fugitives—it is not seemly for the weak to be bold in speech.

So in his concluding words he hints at some of the difficulties of a woman's life:

I charge you, bring me not to shame, you whose youthful bloom is so attractive to men. Ripe tender fruit is never easy to protect; men are like animals, they seek only to destroy. Your gardens fair, the lady of love herself proclaims their dewy freshness, and when a virgin comes in dainty loveliness every man as he passes by falls victim to desire, and shoots a swift glance to win her fancy. . . . Observe, then, this your father's charge, and value chastity more then life itself.

The *Suppliant Women* presents one particular phase of women's subjection considered impersonally, and scarcely deals with the great question of how far force may be rightly met by force. In the legend the daughters of Danaus escape from slavery by killing their husbands on their wedding night, but of that Æschylus in this play tells us nothing.

The problem, however, is too vital to escape his notice, and it forms the central motive of the greatest play in world-literature, the *Agamemnon*. 'Is a woman ever justified in killing her husband?' The question had a special interest in Athens, as it must have in any society where women are kept enslaved, for the tyrant always walks in dread of the assassin's knife. Euripides, with his stinging irony, reveals the secret fear: 'If women are to be allowed to shed male blood,' he makes Orestes cry, 'then we men had better commit suicide at once; if it is a matter only of the will to kill, we may be sure that all women have that already.' The *Agamemnon* deals with this problem ; the sequel plays with a second question, 'Is it right for a son to kill his mother in order to avenge his father's death ? '

But the trilogy of the *Oresteia*, besides being concerned with feminist problems, is a living gallery of woman types : Clytemnestra and Cassandra, Electra and the Nurse, the chorus of maidens in the *Choephoroi*, and the chorus of women furies in the *Eumenides*. In the *Agamemnon* the two women are sharply contrasted ; Clytemnestra, the queen who will not submit to man's rule ; Cassandra, the victim predestined by fate to suffer the caprices of a master, and to pass from the treacherous lover, Apollo, to the brutal owner, Agamemnon. No one can read the play and feel much sympathy with the murdered king. He is done to death with every circumstance of horror ; returning home after many years' absence in a foreign land, where he has been fighting for his country, he finds within his house not a faithful wife, but a secret enemy ; she conceals her hatred, allures him to the bath, and there, with her own hands, murders him.

And yet the dramatist, and his readers, find the wife rather than the husband the sympathetic character. It is partly the intolerable callousness and brutal pride of Agamemnon, who has sacrificed his daughter's life to help on his political schemes, and now brings home with him from Troy the concubine whom he has compelled to share his bed. But there is also the feeling that Clytemnestra is really the better man of the pair : that she is naturally born to rule, and that her subjection to a man would be against the law of nature. Certainly in the play she takes the first place, and Cassandra, a part vocally the most important of any, comes next. The men, Agamemnon, the Watchman, the Herald, Ægisthus, and the helpless chorus of aged councillors, are merely foils to the 'manlike' queen. The contrast, indeed, between the resolute woman and the irresolute men in the closing scenes is almost comic, and the play ends with her triumph. In the sequel, *The Libation Bearers*, the main action is again in the hands of women, Electra and her friends, the maidens of the chorus. Orestes, it is true, does the actual killing ; but there is this difference between brother and sister : Electra acts on her own initiative, and is a woman as strong-willed as Clytemnestra herself ; Orestes acts only in obedience to the promptings of others. Electra feels no remorse ; Orestes, as soon as he has killed his mother, is tormented by imaginary terrors. Among the characters of the second play, by far the most interesting is the old Nurse. She is obviously studied from the life, and is one of the most vivid figures of Greek Drama : her kindly temper and affection for her former charge are contrasted with the fierce bitterness of Electra, and she supplies the one touch of humour that lightens the mournful music of this play.

Last comes the *Eumenides*, which discusses with almost embarrassing frankness the physical problems of relationship. 'Is the mother who conceives, or the father who begets the child, the nearer relative?' And again, 'Is not the murder of a husband, who is no relation by blood, less heinous than the murder of the mother who brought you into the world?' These are some of the questions that are raised but not answered, for the final reconciliation satisfies the religious rather than the practical sense. The plot may be put briefly:

A band of women are pursuing a man over the earth; pursuing relentlessly until he shall die of fatigue. Whenever the pursuit slackens, another woman—or rather her spirit—urges on the chase. The man appeals in vain for help from men, and at last a third woman by skilful diplomacy persuades the avengers—or at least some of them—to agree to a reconciliation.

Such is the Æschylean theatre; but, as we have said, Æschylus is a lonely spirit in Athens. The general view of women is represented by the next generation, Pericles, Sophocles, and Thucydides, the greatest statesman, dramatist, and historian of their time. The last of the three is particularly significant. You may read through his History from beginning to end—and if you are a student of affairs you will not find any other book in the world quite so valuable—but, concerning one-half of the human race, you will get scarcely a word. Even in the hortatory speeches, when soldiers are being encouraged to fight for their possessions, women only come in the second place after the children. In the rest of the History they are practically never mentioned.

To Thucydides, women, even such a woman as Aspasia, hardly existed. Politics were to him the serious business, war the great game of life, and in neither of these did women take part. He probably would have agreed with his hero Pericles, ' a woman's highest glory is not to fall below the standard of such natural powers as she possesses : that woman is best of whom there is the least talk among men, whether in the way of praise or blame.'

In his indifference the historian faithfully follows the example of the statesman. Pericles, of whose mistress, Aspasia, we hear so much, and of whose wife, the mother of his sons, we hear so little, appears never to have considered the part that nature has assigned to women in the creation and management of a state. In his day Athens was faced by a war that in one year robbed her of many of the bravest of her sons. A state funeral was given them at which, as Thucydides tells us : ' Any one who wished, stranger or citizen, could be present: even women were there to mourn for their relatives at the grave.' At the end of the ceremony Pericles made that Funeral Oration in praise of Athens of which echoes are to be found in all contemporary Greek literature. Most of the speech dwells resolutely on the glory of these heroic deaths and the grandeur of the sacrifices made, but at the last the orator condescends to human feeling and addresses some noble words of comfort to the men before him, taking them in succession as fathers, sons, and brothers of the dead. Then comes the one final cold sentence addressed not to the mothers, but to the widows in his audience: 'a few words of advice,' Pericles calls it, and it is the language of reproof rather than that of sympathy.

Their ignorance of women made even the greatest minds in Athens insensible to women's true position, and in the case of Thucydides there is a further reason. When the historian came to compose his work he was too bitterly disillusioned to concern himself with anything but his main subject, the failure of Athens to maintain the Periclean system. In a world where blind chance seemed to rule and the highest political ideals went unrealised, the social position of women may well have seemed to him a trifle.

But Thucydides' testimony is chiefly negative:

we get clearer evidence from Sophocles. Sophocles is the typical Athenian, versatile and ingratiating, '*eutrapelos, eukolos.*' Actor, poet, priest, and general, he was one of the most popular men of his time—*with men.* Of his family life we have not quite such a brilliant picture. His wife is one of the many anonymous women, the wives of great men. His children did not apparently regard their father with as much affection as did the outside world, and in his old age tried to deprive him of the control of his property. As to women, and the softer affections of life, outside his own writing we have the anecdote in Plato's *Republic.* The poet in his old age was asked how he felt in regard to love: 'Hush, hush,' he replied; 'I have escaped and right gladly. I feel like a slave who has escaped from a mad master.'

That was the feeling which the conditions of life at Athens engendered. Woman and woman's love was a necessary weakness: happy the man who could break free, and if we believe the stories in Athenæus, Sophocles also in escaping from women fell into the Ionian snare. In his plays women are generally a negligible quantity; at least the only women whom he succeeds in making lifelike are the slave women, the ministering angels like Deianira and Tecmessa who meekly respect their master's words, 'oft dinned into their ears'—'Woman, for women silence is the finest robe.'

Tecmessa, beautiful character though she is, and far superior to Ajax in moral strength, has no independent existence apart from her lord and master. Deianira, deserted by her errant husband, has no thought of resentment: she only wants to get her master back, and is prepared to stoop to any means if she may regain his company. And it is obvious that these two ladies, who would make a modern woman despair, are Sophocles' ideals of feminine excellence.

Of the other plays, the *Œdipus Tyrannus* contains only one woman character—Jocasta; the mother married to her own son, a dreadful figure, and one almost impossible to dramatise successfully. In the play she takes only a minor part, and her silent exit is the most effective touch; but it is interesting here to compare Sophocles with Euripides, who in the *Phœnician Women* does succeed in making Jocasta a real and most pathethic figure. The *Œdipus at Colonus* has the two girls, Antigone and Ismene, but they are sexless and dramatically only important as types of girlish devotion. The *Philoctetes*, like the two Œdipus plays, has a male chorus and alone among Greek tragedies, if we except the *Rhesus*, has no female characters. It is also, whatever the reason, the dullest play we possess.

There remain the *Electra* and the *Antigone*, and the first of these is a signal example of the importance for a dramatist of choice of subject. Æschylus and Euripides have both left us plays dealing with the same story, and a comparison with the three tragedies will reveal the essential differences between the three poets. A dramatist must share—imaginatively at least—in his characters' thoughts; and women like Clytemnestra and Electra were so beyond the range of Sophocles' experience and sympathy that he is quite unable to make them live. Like everything that Sophocles wrote, the *Electra* is full of literary accomplishment. The epic method, for example, is most ingeniously adapted to the theatre, and a vivid narrative of the chariot race in which Orestes is supposed to meet his death forms the centre of the play, but there is no real grip on the dramatic situation: it is literature, not life.

In the *Antigone*, on the other hand, the poet is dealing with a subject thoroughly congenial to his temperament, the conflict between law and the individual, and one independent of sex, and the play is a magnificent example of his art.

Here certainly the central figure is a woman, or, at least, a girl; but the interest does not depend upon her sex, for little dramatic use is made of the Hæmon episode. It is not her sex but her social position that affects the problem of the play, a problem vital enough in itself without any sex interest—' How far is an individual justified in setting his or her conscience against the law of the State ? '

Antigone is a girl orphan, born out of legal wedlock, a slave without a master ; and it is a crowning stroke of irony to pit her lonely figure against the majesty of man-made law. To modern readers she seems intensely pathetic, and an Athenian audience would, doubtless, have sympathised with her as a rebel, if not as a woman. There is no word in Greek for ' to command,' and their only word for ' to obey ' means literally ' to allow oneself to be persuaded,' so that the conscientious objector was not uncommon. But Sophocles had been a general, and knew by experience the way of Athenian soldiers, and it is not certain that he appreciates his heroine's wilfulness in quite so favourable a light ; for, as we see in his other plays, he was essentially on the side of law. He was rather an observer, with a wonderful command of language, than an original thinker or critic of the established order ; and it is a curious turn of fortune for a poet, who had by no means a close or a sympathetic knowledge of woman's character, that the *Antigone*, the only play where a woman takes a vital part, should be by far the greatest of his works.

The titles and fragments of his lost plays confirm the impression given by the extant tragedies. We have nearly a hundred names of lost plays, and barely one-fifth are called after women. Moreover, a consideration of the titles of those plays that bear one woman's name will reveal the fact that the majority were probably rather anti-feminist than feminist. Helen, Eriphylë, Pandora, Procris, Tyro: Helen, who deserted her husband and her home; Eriphyle, who sold her husband for gold; Pandora, the incarnate cause of trouble among men; Procris, bought by a paramour; Tyro, seduced by a second lover: the legends of these ladies were arranged to please the Athenian public. Venal and fickle creatures, they show plainly how necessary it is to keep a close guard over women, and it may be suspected that Sophocles, in his treatment of the plot, did not disappoint the expectations of his audience.

In five plays only is the title taken from the chorus, the *Spartan Women*, the *Lemnian Women*, the *Water-carriers*, the *Women of Scyros*, and the *Captive Women*; and it is very unlikely, considering the titles, that any one of the five was written with much sympathy with feminine ideals. 'Spartan' and 'Lemnian' women were at Athens almost proverbial for 'unwomanly' females; a 'Water-carrier' was synonymous with a gossip. Of the other two we have a little definite information. Philostratus tells us that the *Women of Scyros* treated of the not very pleasant tale of the young Achilles, disguised as a girl in the king's harem, and becoming there the father of Neoptolemus, by the young princess,

Deidameia. Of the *Captive Women* we know that it had the same plot as Euripides' *Trojan Women,* but the incidents were treated—*humorously.* It is not, perhaps, impossible that an author even to-day might regard the troubles of women in war as a fit subject for a jest ; but things have advanced so far that we should hardly regard him now as a flawless genius, or hold him up as the highest product of our civilisation.

VII.—Euripides

All Greek literature has one peculiar quality. As the tribe of scholiasts and translators have found from the beginning, it lends itself to interpretation; and Euripides has suffered more than most authors from his interpreters. The ancient belief that Euripides was a misogynist is still sometimes held, and such a misconception is not altogether our own fault. It is partly due to Euripides himself, for the poet's favourite weapon is irony, and irony is a double-edged sword which can be turned against those who dare to use it. Euripides does not say plainly and straightforwardly 'You men think yourselves naturally superior to women: braver, more truthful, more unselfish: in reality this superiority is a mere figment of your imagination.' Neither the poet nor his audience would have cared for such brutal frankness. Euripides exhibits the facts of life, with some little malicious arrangement, and leaves the judgment to others. He is too good an artist, as indeed were Æschylus and Sophocles, to make all his women angels and all his men the reverse. Many of his women have very obvious faults, so that if you come to his plays with a fixed and comfortable conviction of the superiority of man, and can shut your eyes to more than half of the action you will probably find in what remains convincing proof of woman's weakness.

But often our belief in Euripides' misogyny has quite another source: our inveterate habit of taking a joke seriously. Aristophanes, who probably knew Euripides—the man and his plays—better than anyone in this world, represents him as a woman-hater in danger from woman's vengeance. We draw the inference that Euripides did really dislike women.

Now the exact opposite of the truth was what the audience at the performance of an Attic comedy expected. It was allowed, it was considered proper in the case of a comic poet, that he should turn his facts upside down. Socrates, for example, always professed himself unable to teach anything and thought the practice of taking fees for teaching immoral. *Therefore,* he is represented in the 'Clouds' as keeping a school and teaching for hire. Euripides is the champion of woman's equality; *therefore,* he is represented by Aristophanes as a misogynist.

There are similar cases in our own social life. An intelligent foreigner, if he read our literature at the time of a general election and took the election posters seriously, would form a very wrong idea of the estimation in which—we will say the Prime Minister—is held by most of his countrymen. A perversion of the facts is even with us regarded as humorous in politics, and it is thus that we should regard Aristophanes. Classical scholars, however, have always been a serious class and while they recognise the grossness of Aristophanes they often fail to see his humour. The irony of Euripides and the humour of Aristophanes are both alien to the Puritan spirit, when they are understood, and to appreciate the first it is necessary to make a close study of all the plays. Euripides was, first of all, a dramatist, and his main business is with his play. But behind the playwright stands the poet and idealist, a man not at all inclined to look on life with philosophic detachment, but feeling, as deeply and as bitterly as any man has ever done, the basis of injustice on which too often human society has been reared.

Euripides championed the cause of woman's freedom against the decadents of Ionia as he championed the cause of religious freedom against the reactionaries of Delphi. He realised that the best method of defence is to attack the other side : that successful defence is impossible, unless at any rate you are prepared to take the aggressive. Open militancy in his case was impossible, for the dramatic poet was ostensibly a servant of the state and the majority, but by no means all, of his countrymen supported the doctrines of the infallibility of the Delphian god and the Athenian man, so that he is compelled to work in exactly the opposite method to that of the misogynists. He does not labour his argument: he does not paint with a heavy brush. If you like to disregard this point of view you can do so, and still find much that is supremely interesting—his gift of vivid narrative, the light music of his verse, and his unrivalled sense of dramatic effect. But every dramatist, consciously or unconsciously, has some groundwork of thought, some criticism of life, which will appear more or less plainly through the dramatic action of his plays. In Euripides that criticism is directed chiefly to the testing of three assumptions current in his day: that God reveals his purposes to men, that war has an ennobling effect on a nation and on individuals, that women are by nature inferior to men.

With the first two of these dogmas we are not now concerned. As to the real nature of Euripides' ideas on the third, we shall get the clearest view if we consider first the characters of his theatre, then the general body of his plays, and lastly, those four dramas which are particularly concerned with the relations between men and women.

The two sexes may be sub-divided, according to

Greek fashion, into six classes: Old man, man, young man, old woman, woman, young woman; and it must be acknowledged at once that Euripides, like most Greeks, is quite lacking in any reverence for age. His old men are apt to be dotards and are treated with humorous contempt. Amphitryon in the Hercules is a type: he lives in a world of illusion: he sees visions and dreams dreams, but when serious counsel or vigorous action are necessary he is useless. Cadmus and Teiresias in the Bacchae are characters of the same sort. They are meant to be humorous, and the scene in which the two old men, wagging their hoary heads, prepare to dance and sing is pure burlesque. Cadmus agrees with Amphitryon in his religious views: he is ready to accept the miraculous, if it is profitable; and he scarcely troubles to make any pretence. As regards the divinity of the new god Dionysus, his sentiments are that, as 'The fellow anyhow is my daughter's son: it is my duty as head of the family to make out that he is a great god'. Cadmus and Amphitryon are at least partly self-deceived; Ægeus is a mere butt. The old gentleman, who believes that his virility can be restored by magic art, is a child in Medea's hands, and the scene between the two is Aristophanic in its outspoken frankness.

Generally speaking, old men in Euripides are impotent: when they are allowed to act, their energies—Tyndareus for example, and the old servant in the Ion—are mischievous. In one case only do old men play a worthy part; when they are resisting the wanton violence of some full-grown man who is attacking women and children. Sometimes, as with Peleus and Iolaus, they succeed; sometimes they fail; but in either case their essential weakness is a foil to the presumptuous strength of their opponent.

Coming now to the second class, that of grown men, we get three main types: there is the mean man, the blusterer, and the simpleton. Jason and Admetus are mean men: mean, selfish and cowardly: capable of asking a woman to save their lives at the risk of her own, but incapable of gratitude. Still they are handsome, good company, and quite unconscious of their own shortcomings. Menelaus is a worse type and one that the poet especially disliked. He adds to meanness the vices of cruelty and treachery and is the slave of passion. In the Orestes he is coldly treacherous, in the Andromache treacherous and cruel, in the other plays where he appears merely despicable. Then come the blusterers: Agamemnon and Heracles, Lycus and Eurystheus. The first two are the ordinary sensual man: brave enough and capable of great deeds, but unfaithful, untruthful and self-indulgent: they seem to be strong, and they are strong in body; but they have no strength of mind. Lycus and Eurystheus are men of a lower type, mere bullies depending solely on force, and Euripides does not attempt to make them interesting. Lastly, there are the simpletons: Xuthus, Thoas and Theoclymenus—an easy prey for the clever women—the Priestess, Iphigenia, Helen who use them as they will. They are the men who with advancing age will be such as Ægeus and Amphitryon. And they almost exhaust the list in our second class. There remain only Theseus, a patriotic abstraction, the male counterpart of Athena; Creon, 'the King'—the name is given to more than one person—an official rather than a living character; and some few persons in the second plan of action: such as the herald Talthybius and the peasant farmer in the Electra. These two latter occupy very subordinate positions, but they are in every way more manly, more generous, more lovable than the great men whom they serve. If we except them, there is not a grown man in the whole theatre of Euripides who can be regarded with sympathy.

When we come to the young men we are in a brighter world. Euripides is essentially the poet of youth, and his younger characters are always lovable. The heroic boy Menœceus and the kind lad Ion are figures drawn with a tender hand. But soon the shadows of the prison house draw in, and the slight hardness which is visible even in Ion becomes intensified in Achilles, and still more in Hippolytus. The older the person, the less attractive he becomes. Achilles and Hippolytus are very much like the public school boy of our day; in many spheres of conduct they are thoroughly reliable: truthful, self-denying and courageous: but they are cruelly hampered by the influence of an environment which shuts out the influence of woman at the most impressionable time of a man's life. Hippolytus is something of a prig and into his mouth, in the well-known speech, Euripides puts all the stock invective against women. The words are not the lad's own views: he is too young to have had much experience of women, good or bad: they are literature, the views of other men expressed in books and unconsciously assimilated by the younger generation.

Hippolytus is an ascetic and exaggerates: Achilles is a more manly character. His first impulses are generous, but he does not carry them into effect, for he is too much under the influence of other people's opinion: 'good form' is his guide in life. He has moreover, all a young man's vanity. 'Countless girls are setting traps to catch me as husband' he says; and he is deeply hurt to think that he is not consulted—'I would have agreed to her death, if I had been asked, but I was not; so I will help you.'

This is the best champion that Clytemnestra can find to save her daughter.

The remaining five characters, men unmarried, but full-grown, are less interesting. Pentheus is the typical 'self-pleaser': wilful, violent and intolerant. That he happens to be right in his particular case does not make him more sympathetic nor does it alter the justice of his fate. His mode of thought is wrong. Savage repression is not the way to deal with a cause which enlists women as its chief votaries and is kept active by their enthusiasm. The other pairs, Orestes and Pylades, Eteocles and Polynices, require little notice. All four have the curse of Cain upon them: they draw the sword and fall by the sword. They are murderers first and foremost, and chiefly interesting to the criminologist.

So much then for Euripides' men. Let us now contrast them in their monotony of type—impute it to the poet or the sex as you will—with the infinite variety of his women: Phædra, Andromache, Hermione, Creüsa, Megara, Helen, Alcestis, Clytemnestra, Medea. There is every shade of conduct here and nearly every form of marital complication, if we remember that none of these wives are in love with their husbands and that romantic affection between husband and wife is impossible. They are all—when they have children—mothers first and wives afterwards; the childless woman—Hermione and, apparently, Creüsa—is embittered by her state and her conduct also is abnormal: she is anxious to take life because she has not given life.

The poet is at pains to show the impossibility of married love under Greek conditions. Phædra is married to an old man, who years before had seduced her sister. Andromache has been forcibly taken by the son of the man who slew her first husband. Hermione has been compelled for political reasons to give up her cousin-lover and marry a stranger. Medea after abandoning everything for her husband is deserted by him. Creüsa has been seduced as a girl and as a 'pis aller' has married an elderly man. Megara has been abandoned by her roving husband: she and her children are on the point of being killed by a stranger when Heracles returns and murders them himself. Helen runs away from her lord; Clytemnestra has no words bad enough to use of hers.

None of these women are impeccable—Alcestis is the only flawless character and she is meant to be a saint—their tempers are as composite as we find them in real life; but, however wrong or mistaken some of their actions may be, not one is altogether unsympathetic. So with the old women. They are sometimes malignant, but they are never contemptible. Their worst deeds are prompted by maternal affection. Phædra's foster-mother is a mischievous and immoral old lady, but her only wish is to gratify her foster child. Hecuba takes a ruthless vengeance on the Thracian king, but she is a mother avenging a murdered son. It is a favourite motive with Euripides ; the pathos of the old mother, her sons killed, her daughters ravished, her grandchildren sold into slavery. Hecuba in the *Trojan Women*, Jocasta in the *Phœnician Women*, the chorus of old women in the *Suppliants* : all represent the reverse side of war's pomp and glory. The men triumph and the women suffer. The method is realistic : there is little romance, in the baser sense of the word, in these unkempt, miserable, old figures, and yet they supply the poet with some of his most poignant passages.

But Euripides is especially successful with his pictures of young girls, virgin martyrs—the type is not extinct—anxious and willing to sacrifice themselves for their male relatives. Iphigenia, Polyxena and Macaria are subtle variations of one character, and upon the figure of the first the poet spends all his skill. At the time of the sacrifice at Aulis she is a sentimental girl, so full of timid modesty that the very thought of marriage fills her with shame. "I hid my face,' she says, 'in the soft wrappings of my veil and would not take my baby brother in my arms nor kiss my sister on the lips—I felt ashamed before them. No, I laid up for myself many a fond embrace which I would give them when I should come back, a married woman.' The arguments she uses to her mother to justify her sacrifice are poor enough: vague talk of honour, patriotism and the insignificance of women—' Tis better that one man should live than ten thousand women'; but her heart is right.

For Iphigenia both marriage and sacrifice prove a delusion. She never returns home; she is defrauded of the joy of motherhood, and spends many years of lonely virginity among strangers and in a strange land. When we see her again she is a bitter woman, more sensible, indeed, than the simple girl, but infinitely less lovable. Her thoughts are all of vengeance: against Menelaus, against Helen, against mankind. She performs her horrible task of human sacrifice with no very great reluctance; 'Parcelling out a tear in sympathy for kindred blood' when any Greek victims fall into her hands; but killing them all the same. For one person alone she still cherishes some affection, her brother Orestes, whom she had left a baby at home, and on him she concentrates her frustrated motherhood.

The final stage of this rancour against life is seen in the character of Iphigenia's sister Electra—' the unwed'—as we have her in the Orestes and the play that bears her name.

Electra's loneliness and suffering, her long brooding, her craving for revenge have turned her mad: she again has only one sound sentiment, her love for her brother. She is a dreadful figure, but a real one. Fire and the knife: murder, treachery, arson: she is ready for all. Her character is the logical outcome of many years of injuries and insults: of denial of rights and of subjection. She is a proud spirit and will not submit, but her pride cannot alter the situation. At last the strain of hopeless rebellion is too great, and she becomes mad.

They make, indeed, a gloomy picture, these unmarried women, for Euripides does not shrink from the darker side of a woman's revolt. As Medea bitterly says 'Even a bad husband is better than none,' and for the unwedded girl there are only two alternatives, a voluntary sacrifice, such as that whereby Macaria escapes from life, or a hopeless struggle against the powers that be, such as Electra tries to wage.

We have now taken all the characters of the Euripidean theatre, except one, and that one the most important of all—the permanent character of tragedy, the chorus.

The chorus is the ideal spectator, the intermediary between audience and actor, the interpreter of the poet's own thoughts. It might be expected that a poet who was a feminist at heart would usually have his chorus composed of women, while a poet who had little sympathy with women would prefer a chorus of men. In our extant plays this is exactly what happens. It is a curious fact that most of the received ideas about the Greek drama; the chorus of elders, the statuesque movements, the dignity of tragedy, etc., etc., are drawn from the theatre of Sophocles, the most academic of the three dramatists: they would never be deduced from the usage of Æschylus or Euripides.

In the seven plays of Æschylus, the chorus is composed five times of women, twice only of men. In both cases they are old men, and the weakness of their old age is necessary to the dramatic action. In Sophocles the proportion is exactly reversed. The chorus is five times composed of men, twice of women. Moreover, it is not the dramatic action that fixes either the sex or the age of the chorus in the Œdipus Tyrannus, the Œdipus Colonus, or the Antigone. In the latter play, indeed, most readers will feel that a chorus of women would be more appropriate; the chorus with Sophocles are old men because the old man is the poet's ideal character.

Of the seventeen plays of Euripides, in only three cases—the Heracles, the Heraclidæ and the Alcestis—is the chorus composed of men. In the first two cases, as in Æschylus, the ineffectiveness of old men in actual danger is part of the plot; the chorus strengthens the impression made by Iolaus and Amphitryon. In the Alcestis, that the chorus are men is part of the general irony of the play.

In the other fourteen plays the chorus is composed of women, and it is into the mouth of these women that Euripides puts all the most intimate part of his work. Sometimes it is a scene of home life as in the Hecuba where a woman describes her last night in Troy.

'It was at midnight that ruin came. Dinner was over and upon men's eyes sweet sleep began to spread. All the songs had been sung: my lord had done with the sacrificial feast and its revelry and was lying in my bower, spear on peg, for no longer had he to keep watch against the throng of shipmen who had set foot on our Ilian land of Troy. As for me, one ringlet of hair I had still to bring to order under my tight-bound snood, and I was gazing into the infinite reflections of my golden mirror ere I should throw myself upon the pillows of my bed. But lo! a cry went through the city and a cheer rang out in Troy-town—"Sons of the Greeks—when, ah when, will you sack the watch tower of Ilion and get you home at last?" Then I fled from my dear couch, with only my smock upon me, like some Dorian maid, and crouched by Artemis' holy shrine. But woe is me, no help found I there. My own man, my bed-fellow, I saw slain before me; and then I was dragged down to the sea shore, and in anguish swooned away.'

Sometimes it is a vivid description of outdoor life, such as the picture of the washing-place, where the humbler sort of women could meet and enjoy a little leisure, 'that pleasant evil,' and gossip together. 'There is a rock that drips, men say, with water from the Ocean's bed and sends from the cliff an ever-running stream, for us to catch in our pitchers. There I met a friend who was washing pieces of fresh-dyed cloth in the river water and laying them in the warm sun upon the flat stones. From her lips first this news of my lady came to me.'

Every mood of a woman's mind is represented: now sad—

> 'Discordant is the music of a woman's life: pitiable helplessness is her lot, an evil housemate, indeed. There is the trouble of child birth, the trouble of woman's weakness.'—(*Hippolytus.*)

or—

> 'A censorious thing is womankind. If women get a small basis for scandal they soon add more. Women take a kind of pleasure in talking insincerely about one another.'—(*Phoenissae.*)

now triumphant—

> 'Children, promise of children's children to be,
> Children to help their sorrow, to make more sweet
> their pleasure,

To speak with their enemy !
Rather, I say, than gold, than a palace of pride,
Give me children at home, right heritors of my blood.
Let the miser plead for the childless side :
I will none of it. Wealth denied,
Children given, I bless them and cleave to the better good.'—(*Ion. Verrall's translation.*)

or—

A strange and wondrous thing for women are the children they bear in travail. Womankind loves a baby.—(*Phoenissae.*)

All the questions of sex are considered and judged with clearest sense.

' Man's love when it is excessive is neither excellent nor, indeed, creditable. But still, sex is a divine thing and a gracious, if kept within bounds. A moderate temper, for that I pray: avaunt, contentious anger and the ceaseless bickering that drives a husband astray to another woman's arms.'—(*Medea.*)

Sometimes the question takes a wider range as in the difficult chorus of the Iphigenia in Aulis.

' The stuff of which men and women are made is different : their ways are different too. But what is really good, of that there is no doubt. The different methods of rearing and education have a great influence on ideas of excellence. Humble modesty is a form of wisdom ; and yet it is wondrous good to use your own judgment and see your duty for yourself. Then life is honourable and your frame grows not old. It is a great thing to seek after excellence. For us women the quest is secret down the secret ways of love; for men the marshalled state and the thronging crowd make a city to increase and prosper.'

But the topic on which Euripides insists most is the scandal of literature, the unfair ideas of woman that have been created and fostered by the perversity of writers. Two quotations will suffice. One from the Ion :—

> ' Ye scandal-masters of the lyre,
> That harping still upon the lust
> Of losel women never tire,
> Her lewdness ever, now be just.
> How doth her faith superior show
> Beside the lust of losel man !
> See it, and change your music. Go
> Another way than once ye ran,
> Ye lyric libels, go, and vex
> The faithless found, the elder sex.'
>
> (*Ion. Verrall's translation.*)

another from the Medea :

' It is men now that are crafty in counsel, and keep not their pledges by the gods ; the scandal will turn and honour come to a woman's life. 'Tis coming—respect for womankind. No longer will pestilent scandal attack women, and women alone. The music of ancient bards will die away, harping ever on woman's perfidy. Phœbus is the guide of melody and in my heart he never set the wondrous music of his lyre. Else I would soon have raised a song that would have stayed the brood of male singers. The long years have many a tale to tell, of men as well as of women.'

This last sentence represents Euripides' reasoned judgment on the problems of feminism. Women are different from men, but they are not inferior : all the arguments that are used to prove woman's weakness could be used equally well against men.

So we may leave the characters and turn now to the separate plays.

Of the complete dramas that we now possess, the Rhesus is probably spurious, the Cyclops is a comic play, the Helena is a burlesque of the tragic manner. Of the remaining sixteen, two, the Suppliant Women and the Children of Heracles, are political plays, written to glorify Athens as the champion of oppressed nationalities, and their interest is manly political. But nothing that Euripides wrote is altogether lacking in vivid touches of feminism. In the Children of Heracles, for example, there is one character who in a few words reveals the position of women in Athenian life : 'For a woman silence and discretion are best, and to remain quiet within doors.' So speaks the maiden Macaria before she consents to a voluntary death. She has had bitter experience of life and she is willing to die, for existence offers her no very pleasant prospect.

'A friendless girl—' she says ' who will take me for

his wife? Who will have children by me? It is better for me to die.' Her one pathetic desire is to die, not on compulsion but as a willing sacrifice, —to escape from life *nobly* (the word recurs as often in Euripides as it does in Ibsen's Hedda Gabler), to leave the ignoble servitude of woman's lot. She begs Iolaus to deal the death-blow and to cover her dead body. But Iolaus, brave old man though he is, cannot bring himself to see her die, and her last request is that at least she may die not among men, but in the arms of women. These are her final words: 'For my people I die. That is my treasure in death: that I take instead of children and my virgin bloom; if indeed anything exists below. I pray for my part that there be *nothing* there: if we mortals who must die shall find life's business in that land also, I know not where to turn. Death is counted the surest potion against pain.'

A similar incident forms the most striking scene of the Suppliant Women. Here it is not a young girl, but a married woman, Evadne, who of her own accord goes to death. But her motive is much the same: 'for the sake of a noble repute I die,' she cries 'that I may surpass all women in generous courage.' Her husband is dead, she is a childless woman, and she refuses to live on as a widow. Her father is anxious that she should nurse him in his old age, but with strange perversity she prefers death and the old man is left to make lament. 'My daughter is dead;' he cries, 'she who used to draw down my face to her lips and would hold my head fast in her arms. Nothing is so sweet as a daughter when a father grows old. A son's life is a thing of greater importance, but sons are not so pleasant when we need fond endearments.'

The main interest of the Suppliant Women is the same as that of three other plays: the Phoenician Women, the Trojan Women, and the Hecuba. They are concerned with war; but war, as seen from the woman's side, a thing of unredeemed and useless suffering. All the 'glory of conquest' disappears: women and children are seen paying the price of men's ambition and pride. The Trojan Women is the most lamentable and the most effective of the series. Written according to the oldest formula of tragedy, the chorus are the chief persons in the action. Hecuba, Cassandra and Andromache are only particular representatives of the sufferings which all the women in the play endure. The two male characters, the lustful hypocrite Menelaus and the honest servant Talthybius are of quite subordinate interest.

The play is an accumulation of sorrow upon sorrow, but the climax is the murder of the little child Astyanax, a political crime, not inspired by any of the human feelings of hatred and revenge, but coldly calculated by men for the sake of future advantage. It is the women, the mother and grandmother of the child, who have to suffer, that men may sleep in safety. As Andromache bitterly says, she has always followed out the whole duty of woman.

'Those things that have been invented as virtuous pursuits for women, at those I laboured ever in Hector's house. To begin with—whether censure should attach to women for it or not, I may not say—but at any rate, the thing in itself brings a woman an evil name when she does not remain ever within doors. So I put aside the desire for going out and stayed at home. Moreover, I never admitted within our house the fantastic talk that some females enjoy: I found my own sound sense the best teacher in domestic matters, and made myself sufficing. A silent tongue and a quiet face—that was what I rendered to my lord.'

And now she has her reward: she is to become a concubine in the house of her husband's murderer, and is told that one night in the arms of her new lord will make her forget the past. As for her baby boy; 'dear youngling nestling in your mother's arms, your skin so sweet and fragrant,' he is torn away and hurled down to death.

But Andromache is not worse treated than the other women. Hecuba is handed over to Odysseus to be his slave, to sweep the floor and grind the daily corn. The virgin Polyxena is reserved to be slain over the tomb of Achilles; for it is not enough that living men should make women their chattels; even the dead hero demands the tribute of a maiden's life. Cassandra has lived a vestal, dedicated to the service of the god, and she too has her reward. The great king deigns to take her to his bed, and in a scene of the grimmest irony the unhappy girl sings her own marriage hymn. There is all the music of the hymeneal chorus, but we have one solitary figure—the unwedded bride—instead of the joyful procession of youths and maidens.

The Hecuba deals with the same events as the Trojan Women and in the same spirit. The sacrifice of Polyxena is consummated and Hecuba takes vengeance on one of her children's murderers, the Thracian king Polymnestor. Beguiled into the captive women's tent he sees his own children murdered and is then blinded. The scene where he comes reeling out with blood-dripping eyes reaches the limits of the horrible, but Euripides does not forget to draw the feminist moral.

'If any one,' the king says, 'has spoken ill of women in the past, or is now in the act of speaking or will some day speak, I will cut all his words short—listen—Neither sea nor land breeds such a race as women are: only the man who has to do with them from time to time knows what they can do.

The unhappy victim of a single woman forgets his logic and imputes the fault of an individual to the sex. If the aggressor had been a man, his thoughts would have been different and so the chorus tell him.

'Be not over-fierce against us nor bring the feminine element into your troubles. There is no need to blame all womankind.'

The particular note of realistic horror that marks the closing scenes of the Hecuba appears in another group of four plays, the Iphigenia in Tauris, the Heracles, the Orestes and the Electra. The first three have been exhaustively studied by Dr. Verrall, and it is enough now to say that the methods of criticism which Thucydides and Euripides use upon the Trojan War, are here applied to other tales of the remote and heroic past. Both writers—the historian and the dramatist—know that human nature does not change, and they strip away remorselessly the glamour of ancient legend. If such things happened, *this* is how they happened, says Euripides; and so we have the half-mad, half-heroic figure of Heracles: the sinister Orestes always ready to unsheath his dagger: the ludicrous yet pitiable Phrygian eunuch stuttering and trembling in panic fear, and most terrible of all the unsexed woman Electra. Each play has its own scene of horror, but the climax, perhaps, comes when

Electra takes the head of the murdered Ægisthus in both hands and pours forth all her bitterness into the deaf ears.

The Hippolytus strikes an entirely different note, and is, perhaps, the best known of all the plays. It has been adapted by Seneca and Racine, used as material by Ovid and transposed into a romantic drama by Professor Murray. But in spite of all this, Phædra's position and motives are often misunderstood. Hippolytus is her natural enemy and the enemy of her children. The bastard son of Theseus, if his father died, would probably oust the legitimate but younger children of the wife from their father's throne and himself seize the power. Phædra, a young woman married to an old husband, is possessed by a physical desire for the young man, but she struggles against her passion *for her children's sake.* When she finally gives up the struggle, she secures her children's safety by ensuring Hippolytus' death or banishment. She knows Theseus and she knows that he will bitterly resent any trespass on his property and punish that trespass with all the severity in his power. The charge is a false one, but it is only thus that her children's future can be protected.

The last two plays, the Bacchæ and the Iphigenia in Aulis, written in old age and in exile at Macedonia, still deal with the double problem, the sacrifice to God and the sacrifice to man; and they are constructed on the same lines.

In the Bacchæ the men are of three sorts. There is the Adept—an imposter, who has taken to religion as a trade; the old men Cadmus and Teiresias who are 'religious' for social and family reasons: finally the young Pentheus who is openly 'irreligious' and comes to a bad end.

The women alone *believe*: they are deceived by the adept, and much of their belief is delusion, but it is a real spiritual benefit—to them. The ritual of Bacchus was the one chance of escape in a Greek woman's life from the stifling seclusion of the harem home. For a few days at least she became a free creature, allowed to roam at large upon the mountains. The thyrsus of the god took the place of her master's company: the sky was her roof: the grass was her bed: she could put aside the wine press and the flour mill and live on milk and honey. The ecstasy of such an escape has never found more intense expression than in the narrative speeches and the choric songs of the Bacchæ.

In the Iphigenia at Aulis the men again are of three types, foils all and each to the idealism of Iphigenia and the practical sense of Clytemnestra. Menelaus is the meanest: the slave of desire, ready for any crime to gratify his passions. Agamemnon is the ordinary middle-aged man, afraid of his wife and fond of his family, but capable of deceiving the one and ruining the other. Achilles is the young man of the governing classes, brought up to despise women, and to think that every girl is anxious to become his wife. The men quarrel and plot for their own selfish ends, but their schemes are detected by the keen wit of Clytemnestra and rendered useless by the unselfish devotion of Iphigenia.

VIII.—Euripides. The Four Feminist Plays

The three main interests of Euripides' mind, realist, pacificist and feminist—to use our ugly jargon—are to be found in all his theatre; but there are four plays which are especially concerned with the relations between women and men, the Alcestis, Medea, Ion and Andromache. They are not pleasant plays: indeed, to a lover of sentimental idealism they would be conspicuously unpleasant if they were fully understood. Nor are they to be recommended to women readers. The relations between the sexes are a delicate thing; and human nature, male humanity at any rate, is generally none the worse for discreet reticence and tender handling. But in these plays Euripides uses the surgeon's knife. They were meant for an audience of men, grown callous by time and custom; and the treatment is ruthless. They should be regarded as the painful but necessary operation, needed to rid a patient of some long-festering ulcer, and the dramatist deserves the thanks that we give to the skilful surgeon.

The particular flaws in the male character with

which Euripides deals in the four plays are these—meanness, cowardice, selfishness, and treachery. They are not the faults, it will be noticed, that are especially appropriate to a ruling class. Man is not indicted on the score of haughtiness, pride or cruelty: his weaknesses are of a less 'manly' sort. It is his position as the natural lord of creation that is questioned and put to the test of dramatic action.

If Jason, Admetus, Apollo and Menelaus are *impossible* characters, then Euripides fails altogether in his lesson: if their actions, though possible, are improbable, then again he fails in an artistic sense. Some may think that no one could be quite so mean as Jason, quite so cowardly and selfish as Apollo and Admetus, quite so treacherous as Menelaus; but if we apply the test of experience, the cruel facts of life will justify the poet. None of the four are 'tragedies,' in the sense in which we use the word. They are as good examples as we are ever likely to see of 'la haute comédie'; the Ion and Andromache, perhaps, a little melodramatic, the Alcestis and the Medea in places almost farcical; but all depending eventually on a subtle study of psychology and social relationships.

It is probable that they were not originally composed for public representation in the great theatre of Dionysus. They are intimate studies of humanity and can quite easily be divested of the official chorus, prologue and epilogue, which are independent of the dramatic action of the play. What is left is Euripides' own teaching, put as plainly as the ironical spirit will allow. The frequency of translation must not blind us to the fact that in essentials Euripides is untranslatable. He is one of the greatest masters of irony and there is nothing that is so apt to vanish in translation, or create confusion in the English mind.

All four plays are concerned with problems of motherhood and children, especially male children. In three, child-actors are required and play an important part in the action: the fourth play, the Ion, has for its hero a lad, just emerging from the 'awkward age' of boyhood.

Between the Ion and the Andromache there is a curious resemblance of plot. The case was probably not uncommon in the circumstances of race-degeneration that prevailed at Athens during the fifth century. In both plays a husband has a childless wife, but a son by an irregular union. There are two women to one man, and in each case there is another man in the background, Apollo who has seduced Creüsa, and Orestes who has been the affianced lover to Hermione. The husbands, Xuthus and Pyrrhus, are the least important figures in the action; indeed, Pyrrhus does not appear in person at all. They are represented as colourless characters; men of position and personal courage, dangerous, perhaps, when roused, but generally negligible. Their young wives, Hermionë and Creüsa, regard them with a mixture of contemptuous fear and jealous affection.

The interest is concentrated on the women, and the plays are studies of wifely jealousy—'Why should my husband have a child, while I am childless?' —and maternal love.

Euripides knows well that motherhood is a woman's natural sphere: a childless woman is for him an abnormal woman, and behaves in an abnormal and anti-social fashion. Both wives attribute their barrenness, probably the natural result of their past history, to supernatural causes. Hermionë believes that the foreign concubine Andromache has bewitched her: Creüsa, that she has incurred the anger of a god. Hermionë accordingly proposes to break the spell by killing the witch; Creüsa goes to Delphi to propitiate the divinity and seek his aid.

Both women, also, in their jealous hate are anxious to kill their husband's bastard. Hermionë uses her father's help and nearly succeeds in murdering the boy Molossus. Creüsa employs her father's old slave as her agent, and all but poisons the boy Ion. In neither case is the crime accomplished, for the plays are not ' tragedies ' ; but the criminal purpose is there. The women have been injured in the past and they are childless. They are embittered against life and ready to requite evil for evil. On the other hand, the unwedded mothers in both plays are ready to sacrifice themselves for their children. Andromache offers her life to save her son—' What pleasure have I in life ? ' she cries, ' In him all my hopes centre : it would be a disgrace for me not to die on behalf of the child I bore. Children, indeed, are life : those who in ignorance disparage them, may feel less pain than we do, but they are miserable in their happiness.'

In the Ion Pythia consents to an even harder sacrifice : she hands over her child to another woman, saves him thereby from the guilt of murder and makes him prince of Athens. Andromache and the Priestess have been injured in the past, but they are saved by their children : the maternal, not the marital, is the holy state.

But in both plays the feminist interest is complicated by other motives, political and religious. In the Andromache a bitter attack is made upon the Spartan system in the person of Menelaus. ' You a man ? ' old Peleus cries, ' You dastard son of dastard parents. What claim have you to be counted among men ? A fine *man* it was, a Phrygian, that robbed you of your wife. You left your hearth and home without a lock, without a servant to guard, as though, forsooth, you had a virtuous wife within doors, she who was the worst of all women. Why, even if she wished, none of your Spartan girls could be virtuous. They leave the shelter of home and go about with young men ; their legs bare, their dresses open ; and run and wrestle like men. It all seems to be abominable. We need not be surprised that your system of education does not produce virtuous women.'

In the Ion the system of Delphi and the oracle is assailed, and a vein of bitter irony runs through the play. So ironical is the poet's method that, if we take the prologue seriously and confine ourselves to the statements there made, we are apt to get a somewhat misleading idea of the play's purpose. Dr. Way, for example, who gives the traditional interpretation with the greatest clearness, supplies the following summary of the action.

'In the days when Erechtheus ruled over Athens, Apollo wrought violence to the king's young daughter Creusa. And she, having borne a son, left him, by reason of her fear and shame, in the cave wherein the God had humbled her. But Apollo cared for him, and caused the babe to be brought to Delphi, even to his temple. Therein was the child nurtured, and ministered in the courts of the God's house. And in process of time Erechtheus died, and left no son nor daughter save Creüsa, and evil days came upon Athens, that she was hard bestead in war. Then Xuthus, a chief of the Achæan folk, fought for her and prevailed against her Eubœan enemies, and for guerdon of victory received the princess Creusa to wife, and so became king-consort in Athens. But to these twain was no child born; so, after many years, they journeyed to Delphi to inquire of the oracle of Apollo touching issue. And there the God ordered all things so that the lost was found, and an heir was given to the royal house of Athens. Yet, through the blind haste of mortals, and their little faith, was the son well-nigh slain by the mother, and the mother by the son.'

This summary quite faithfully represents the statements of the divine Hermes; but Euripides knows as well as we do that gods do not walk the earth and that children are not miraculously wafted through the air. The prologue satisfies convention: the play itself is realistic and one of the chief characters is a woman of whom the prologue tells us nothing. The real plot, as opposed to the idealistic version, is as follows:—the facts are put down crudely instead of being conveyed by subtle hints and innuendo as they are in the Greek.

A young Athenian girl, Creüsa, wandering one day alone in the fields is attacked by a brutal satyr. He drags her into a cave, violates her and then makes his escape. She faints, and on awakening imagines that her assailant, who has disappeared as suddenly as he came, was a being from another world: she had seen him in the full sunlight; he is the sun-god Apollo. She tells no one of her adventure, conceals her condition and when her time comes, makes her way alone to the same cave. The child is born, wrapped by the girl mother in a piece of cloth, and placed, together with a golden bracelet as token, in a wicker basket. Then he is abandoned, and of his fate we hear no more.

About the same time at Delphi, in one of those periods of promiscuous sexual intercourse allowed and encouraged by temple ritual, one of the Delphian women becomes a mother, by a roving soldier of fortune named Xuthus. The latter leaves Delphi, ignorant of his paternity, and the woman is soon after appointed priestess of the temple. Her child, Ion, ostensibily a foundling, is reared within the temple precinct and regards the priestess as his foster mother. Meanwhile, the soldier Xuthus makes his way to Athens and marries Creusa. They have no children, and come to Delphi to ask advice of the oracle. The priestess recognises Xuthus as the father of her son, and so arranges matters—remaining herself unseen—that after a conversation with the boy he acknowledges him as his child, the result of the former hasty connexion.

But though Xuthus has now got a son, Creüsa is still a childless wife. In passionate anger she reveals her long hidden secret, denounces the god as the author of her ruin, and with the help of a slave, attempts to poison Ion. The plot fails, she is pursued as a murderess by Ion and is on the point of being put to death. Then the priestess once more intervenes. She has heard Creüsa's story—in some details not unlike though more lamentable than her own—and she determines to help a fellow sufferer. She has already given up her son to his father, and she now arranges a second trick whereby Creüsa shall believe Ion to be her child. She has in her possession a baby's wicker cradle, a piece of cloth similar to that in which the dead baby was wrapped, and Creüsa's own bracelet which has been used in the poisoning plot. By an ingenious subterfuge she makes all three appear to be the recognition tokens of Creüsa's child. Creüsa with joy, Ion with some painful doubts, accept the new relationship; and so the play ends.

The Ion and the Andromache both abound in incident: the Medea and the Alcestis depend more on a psychological interest. They are 'one-part' plays—the strong woman Medea and the weak man Admetus—and they have many points of resemblance. In the Medea a mother kills her children to save her own pride: in the Alcestis a mother consents to death to save her children's position. Alcestis is a saint: Medea—to some people—a devil.

Medea is certainly not meant to be a pleasant character. She has laboured too long under a sense of injustice to be pleasant either in her thoughts or behaviour. 'You are always abusing the government;' Jason says to her, 'and so you will have to be ejected.' She expresses the revolt of women in its bitterest form. 'Of all things that draw breath,' she cries, 'and have understanding, we women are the most miserable; we are merely *a thing that exists.* To begin with, we must outbid each other to buy ourselves a lord and take a master of our body. 'Tis a risky business—we may get a knave or an honest man. To leave her husband brings a woman no honour, and we may not refuse our lords. When a woman comes to fresh ways and pastures new, she needs must be a prophet, for she has never been taught at home how best to use the man who now shares her bed. If we work our task aright, and our lord keeps house with us, and does not kick against the yoke, then our life is enviable. If not—better to be dead. A man, if he is vexed with the company of his household, goes out and purges away his heart's annoyance; but we women are compelled to look ever at one soul.'

This isolation was the worst feature in a Greek woman's life : to a clever woman it was soul-destroying, and Medea is incomparably cleverer than any man in the play. The scenes where she forces the two old men, 'King' Creon and 'King' Ægeus to do, not what they want, but what she wants, are masterpieces of satirical humour. With her husband her cleverness fails her : she is too angry to reason : she hisses her scorn and foams her disgust. Jason keeps cool and so far has the best of the argument.

'You certainly are a clever woman,' he says, 'but you are only a woman. I am a very fine figure of a man : you fell in love with me ; and it was only natural.'

Jason is in many ways like Admetus. Both are lovers of outward show and have a great regard for men's opinion. Both say with some emphasis that a family of two children is quite large enough. Both have the same opinion of women ; and this is how Jason concludes—'Men ought to be able to get their children from some other source : the female sex should not exist : and then there would be no trouble for mankind.'

Such sentiments naturally fail to please either the chorus or Medea. The comment of the chorus is, 'You have made the best of your case, but still, surprising though it may seem to you, I think you are acting unfairly in betraying the woman who has shared your bed.' Medea gives full vent to her anger: she contemptuously refuses the help in money which Jason says he is 'ready to give with an ungrudging hand,' and at last scornfully dismisses him—'Be off with you. You are yearning for the new girl you have broken in, all the time that you linger outside her house. Go and play the bridegroom with her.'

But in the next scene Medea has mastered her temper and pretends to submit. 'We are but what we are,' she says, 'just women. You must not take pattern by the evil nor answer folly with foolishness. I give way: I acknowledge that I was wrong.' Jason is patronising and friendly in his answer: 'I approve your present attitude, and, indeed, I do not blame your past behaviour: it is only to be expected: woman is a thing of moods.' He consents to ask his new wife for a remission of the children's exile. 'Certainly I will, and I fancy that I shall persuade her.' 'Yes, indeed, you will,' Medea says, 'if she is one of us: all women are alike. But I will help you once again in this enterprise, too.' And as in the past she had given him an antidote against the fire-breathing bulls, so now she gives him the fiery robe which is to destroy the young bride.

Then comes the crucial scene of the play: Medea

kills her children and we are faced by the problem—when is killing murder?

A mother who kills her child is to us a dreadful figure, and the death penalty is invoked against the deserted girl-mother: no punishment is inflicted upon the father, perhaps because no punishment can be adequate. Greek law and custom went further and in a different direction. The father was allowed to decide whether the child whom his wife had brought forth should be reared. Child killing in this fashion, when done by the father, was not a crime, and the exposure of children after birth was a common, and by no means held to be a reprehensible act. Plato, indeed, thinks it a fit subject for a jest in the Theætetus (p. 161). 'Do you think,' says Socrates, 'that it is right in all cases to rear your own child? Will you be very angry if we take it—the argument—from you, as we might take a baby from a young mother with her first child?' 'Oh, no,' answers the other. 'Theætetus will not mind: he is not at all hard to get on with.'

The mother who did mind was regarded as a difficult person, but whether she minded or not, decision lay with the father—as we see in Terence's play, The Self Tormentor. There the wife says to her husband, 'You remember, don't you, when I was pregnant, you told me emphatically that if the child should be a girl you would refuse to rear it.' The child proved to be a girl, and so without further question it was got rid of. Male children were more valuable, and unless the circumstances of their birth were exceptional, as in the case of Paris and Œdipus, they were not often exposed.

There is this further point: what differentiates killing from murder is the question of risk. You kill, you do not murder, when you risk your own life. A soldier is not a murderer, and in sport a fox-hunter is a man of different type from a pigeon shooter. Now the Athenian women were not Amazons, but they fought a battle no less dangerous. 'They say of us,' cries Medea, 'that we live a life free from danger within doors, while men are fighting like heroes with the spear. But men are fools. Rather would I stand three times in the battle line of shields than bear one child.' A mother had already risked her life in bringing a child to birth; is she not far more justified than the father in ending that child's life, if such be her will? Moreover, children are the pledges of marriage, the securities given for a business arrangement. Is it right that the party who wilfully breaks the compact should retain possession of the securities?

Such I believe are some of the questions that Euripides meant to suggest. It is no answer to them to say that it is an unnatural crime for a mother to kill her children, for it is equally unnatural and criminal for a father, and yet ancient fathers killed their children without compunction and without blame.

The Medea then is realistic and little else: the Alcestis, the first in time of Euripides' plays, is a blend of style, and demands a fuller treatment.

There are no villains in the Alcestis, and there are no heroes. There is one heroic character, but her heroism is of so common a type that it usually passes unnoticed. The three men, Admetus, Pheres and Heracles, in varying degrees are animated by the strongest of all male motives, self-preservation. Alcestis lacks their sound common-sense; she is guided by passion, by the strongest of all female passions and that which comes nearest to the divine, the maternal passion of self-sacrifice. She has given life once, she is prepared to give it again.

It is commonly assumed—and even Verrall tacitly allows this to go unchallenged—that Alcestis 'is in love with' Admetus, and Admetus 'is in love with' Alcestis. The affection which, happily for us, may usually be expected to exist between husband and wife, is taken for granted in the very different conditions of Euripides' time.

Now, as we have seen, this is a cardinal error. Mutual affection and esteem did *not* reign in an ordinary Athenian household. Husband and wife were usually indifferent one to another, and even this indifference was an improvement upon the Ionian relationship when husband and wife were often natural enemies.

That a wife should give up her life out of love for her husband is a state of things so agreeable to the natural man that it is, perhaps, not surprising if the language of the play has never been too closely examined.

Alcestis' motive is not love for her husband, but love for her children. Euripides, following Æschylus, knew that maternal love is a far stronger force than conjugal affection, even when the latter exists. The mother and the children—on them he spends all the resources of his unrivalled pathos—the husband is a mark for his bitterest irony. It is because Alcestis does not wish her children to be left *fatherless* that she consents to death.

The position of the widow—as indeed, is implied in our language by the form of the word—is definitely worse than that of the widower. The orphan in ancient times was the fatherless child, and the position of the chief's son whose father died in his childhood was particularly unenviable. It is described in two of the most pathetic passages in Greek literature, by Andromache in the twenty-second book of the Iliad and by Tecmessa, in the most Euripidean of all the plays of Sophocles, the

Ajax. Under the old tribal system, a chief's power depended very largely on personal ascendency, so that old men like Laertes and Pheres found it expedient to retire in favour of their grown-up son. A small boy like Eumelus could not have maintained his father's position, and his father's death would probably have meant considerable danger to his life. All this in Euripides' time was a commonplace and needed no emphasis. He prefers, indeed, to deal with the reverse picture—the sorrows of the motherless children and especially of the motherless girl; for the pathos of the sacrifice is partly this. It is for the sake of the boy and his future position in life, and not so much for the girl, that the mother dies.

Let us now examine the play itself. Admetus, chief of Pheræ, has been told by his medicine man that he is a very bad life: that, indeed, he cannot hope to live much longer—three months, perhaps; six months, say, at the most. But he has been a generous benefactor to the profession, and in particular has rendered some quite exceptional services to the arch-physician, Apollo himself. Accordingly a special provision is made in his case. If he can get some one of his own family to transfer to him their vitality, the operation may be feasible. The problem is, to find the man—or woman—for his family is very small. Admetus goes to his father and his mother, but both, even his mother, refuse; for, as we shall see, Admetus is not a very sympathetic character, or likely to arouse the spirit of self-sacrifice even in a mother's heart. Finally he asks his young wife, the mother of his two little children, and she consents.

At this point the play opens. Admetus believes what he is told; Alcestis believes what she is told: the sixth month is ending and she is marked out for death. So Death appears, and the burlesque dialogue between Death and the Doctor, Thanatos and Apollo, forms the prologue, where the arch-physician, who can cure all diseases but one, is confronted by that One himself. But the prologue and the entrance of the chorus need not detain us. The first intimate details about Alcestis are given by the servant woman in her long speech to the chorus, and it will be noticed that in the picture of the household which she draws for them the central point is the marriage bed. Twice already has Alcestis risked her life upon that bed, and now another sacrifice has to be made. A childless woman might refuse. Her husband demands her life, and she must give it for the sake of the children whom on that bed she has borne. It is of her children that Alcestis thinks: for them she prays: she has no petition to make on her husband's behalf. In all the narrative, indeed, the husband scarcely appears. The chorus

—*of men*—notice the omission and enquire of him, and this is the answer they get :

'*Oh, yes he is weeping* as he holds the woman he loves, his bedfellow, in both arms. He is begging her not to abandon him : *he wants what he cannot have.*'

The chorus then burst into a lament which is interrupted by the appearance of Alcestis and her husband outside the house. The following scene is an extreme example of that combination of pathos and irony from which Euripides never shrinks. The lamentation of Alcestis, expressed in lyrics of the purest quality, is answered at regular intervals by Admetus in iambic couplets where style and thought alike are cruelly commonplace.

Then Alcestis who has been standing, supported by her women, sinks to the ground and with one last cry *to her children* thrice repeated seems to faint away. Admetus in the name *of the children* begs her not to forsake him 'this is worse *for me* than any death : on you we all depend—to live or die.' Alcestis makes her final effort, and for the first time addresses her husband by name, but in the pathetic speech that follows, her last words are for her children, and it is plain that she is terribly afraid that Admetus will marry again and inflict a step-mother upon them. Admetus himself hesitates to give the promise, and it is one of the chorus who answers the dying wife.

With Alcestis disappears the pathos of the play. The rest is ironical, a realistic criticism of the resurrection story and hardly concerns us. But the scene between Pheres and Admetus where the old father—the mother is prudently omitted from the action,—comes to convey his sympathy, is a beautiful illustration of Euripides' insight into the weakness of the male character.

'Such are the pair, father and son: behold your ordinary sensual man,' he seems to say. Dr. Verrall spends some time and pains in showing that Admetus is not a hero, and, doubtless, he is not heroic either to us or to Euripides. But it does not follow that an Athenian audience would share our or the master's private views. We are unconsciously influenced by centuries of romantic literature in which the relations of the sexes have been idealised. The Athenians treated women much as the baser sort still treat animals. To us Admetus seems almost inconceivably selfish and callous: probably many an Athenian never realised that his conduct was reprehensible.

Even so to-day a vegetarian has considerable difficulty in proving to the ordinary man that it is unjustifiable selfishness to take life for the gratification of appetite. 'I always have eaten meat,' such an one will say; 'I always shall: and so did my father. Animals were created for use.' The Athenian might have used the same language about his wife.

But in the play itself no one is under any sort of delusion as to Admetus. The servant woman, the attendant, the chorus, Alcestis herself: all know him for what he is, a selfish coward. Very religious certainly he is and very hospitable: in other words, very full of absurd superstitions and very fond of having strangers in the house to divert him from himself. Heracles the ravisher, and Apollo the seducer, appreciate him as an excellent boon companion: his own household do not share their views. They know too well—and there is constant reference to this in the play—that he is 'foolish' in the Euripidean sense of the word, the slave of passions which he is unable to control. And so we may leave him: in his character Euripides explodes the fallacy that in all cases and in all circumstances man is the superior animal.

But the wonder of the Alcestis is this: in spite of the irony and cruel satire, in spite of the bitter criticism of the two doctrines, the existence of the supernatural and the superiority of man, there remain so many other threads of interest—realism and romance, pathos and humour—that a well-disposed reader can shut his eyes to the unpleasant, and usually does. What is wanted to bring out the full meaning of Euripides' plays is a double translation ; one version written in prose by a realist with a taste for irony, the other composed by a lyric poet. Neither version will be satisfactory apart, for the spirit of Euripides is a compound of the two : neither will be final, for translations quickly age and Euripides is ever young.

IX.—The Socratic Circle

Sophocles is almost the last representative of the earlier and happier period of the Athenian Empire, their golden age as it seemed later, when to the complacent imagination of the male citizen all things seemed to be working together in the direction of progress and freedom. Progress indeed there was, and for men freedom of thought, for the intellectual atmosphere of Athens in the middle of the fifth century B.C., with its combination of clear knowledge and bracing speculation, has never been surpassed. But as a society, Athens already contained within herself the seeds of decay and destruction. The wealth of her intellectual achievement barely concealed the poverty of her social morality, and it was only by dint of firmly closing their eyes to the degradation of their women and the misery of their slaves that the Athenians maintained for a time the fond illusion that everything was for the best in the best of all possible cities.

Then came the shock of the Peloponnesian War and the inherent weaknesses of a free State which refuses political freedom to more than half its population were cruelly revealed. For nearly thirty years, with some few breathing spaces, the struggle went on, while Athens tried to force a culture intellectually superior but morally inferior to that of many other of the Greek peoples upon a reluctant world: and in the end she failed and fell.

After the fifth century the political importance of Athens disappears; her intellectual pre-eminence is saved for her by a small group of men who under the hard teaching of war discerned the flaws of her social system and set themselves resolutely to the task of criticism and reform. The nobility of war, the nobility of birth, the nobility of sex: these are some of the prejudged questions that the Socratic Circle ventured to dispute, and their contentions, as we have them recorded in the literature of the late fifth and the early fourth centuries, form perhaps the most valuable legacy that the Greek mind has left us. But, like so much of Greek thought, their ideas require interpretation for a modern reader. Some of the greatest of the Circle, Socrates and Antisthenes, for example, we only know in the writings of other men, and we have to disentangle the master's ideas from those of his disciples. Plato and Xenophon were drawn away by metaphysics and soldiering, and social problems form only a part of their interests. Euripides and

Aristophanes were compelled to conform to the conventions of Attic tragedy and comedy, and we must always discount the influence of the stage; Euripides is often less and Aristophanes more serious than suits our ideas of a tragic and a comic writer. Lastly, for all the group except Xenophon, irony was the favourite weapon of attack, an irony so deftly veiled that it made the bitterest criticism possible, and still often passes undetected.

But even so the critics were not popular and their reforms were not accepted: Socrates was put to death; Plato found a shelter in political obscurity; Euripides, like Æschylus, passed much of his life away from Athens; Xenophon took up his home in the Peloponnese: in their lives they fought against a stubborn majority, and when they were dead the social organisation of Athenian life remained apparently unchanged. But their teaching lived on after them, and on feminist questions it derives almost an additional value from the general hostility of their fellow-countrymen.

In their criticism of the problems that we call feminism Euripides and Socrates were the initiative forces, and a close study of the former's plays is indispensable for any one who wishes to understand the position of women in Athenian life. But the plays of Euripides throw also a certain light on the position of Socrates himself. Socrates and

K

Euripides we know were close friends: 'which of the two gathered the sticks and which made the faggot,' so runs the ancient saying, 'no man can tell,' and in many points of family relationship they had the same experience. Euripides' mother, Cleito 'the greengrocer,' Socrates' wife, Xanthippë 'the scold,' are two of the rare women in Athenian history of whom we know even the names. Both men were lovers of women in the nobler sense, and the later misogynists revenged themselves by enlarging upon their marital infelicities. In the case of Euripides there is no real evidence to support these scandals, and even if Xanthippë was a woman of strong temper, both men were well enough satisfied with the married state to take another wife in addition to their first helpmate, when a special law, rendered necessary by the waste of male lives in the great war, gave formal sanction to such a step. Both alike agreed in condemning the misogyny of their day and knew that a man who habitually thinks ill of women has probably no very good reason to think well of himself. Both applied to women as well as to men the great doctrines of liberty, equality, fraternity.

Euripides saw in woman the equal and not the slave of man, Socrates regarded her as his natural friend and not his natural enemy. In Xenophon's Socratic books, the *Memorabilia*, the *Œconomicus*, and the

Symposium, we get the best record of the master's view of the women, for Socrates was himself too cautious ever to commit himself to the written word, and perhaps the most characteristic of the episodes is the visit to the fair hetaira, the one faithful of all the lovers of Alcibiades, described in the *Memorabilia.*

There lived in Athens a fair lady called Theodotë, whose habit it was to give her society to any one who could woo and win her. One of the company made mention of her to Socrates, remarking that the lady's beauty quite surpassed description. 'Painters,' said he, 'go to her house to paint her portrait, and she displays to them all her perfection!' 'Well,' said Socrates, 'manifestly, we too must go and see her. It is impossible from mere hearsay to realise something which surpasses description.' Thereupon his informant: 'Quick, then, and follow me.'

So off they went at once to Theodotë, and found her at home, posing to a painter. When the painter had finished, 'Friends,' said Socrates, 'ought we to be more grateful to Theodotë for displaying to us her beauty, or she to us for having come to see her? I suppose if this display is going to be more advantageous to her, she ought to be grateful to us. But if it is we who are going to make a profit from the sight, then we ought to be grateful to her.' 'Very fairly put,' said one, and Socrates resumed, 'The lady is profiting this moment by the praise she receives from us, and when we spread the tale abroad she will gain a further advantage. But, as for ourselves we are beginning to have a desire to touch what we have just now seen: when we are going away we shall feel the smart, and after we have gone we shall still long for her. So we may reasonably say that it is we who are the servitors, and that she accepts our service.' Thereupon Theodotë: 'Well, if that is so, it would be only proper for me to thank you for coming to see me.' Afterwards Socrates noticed that the lady herself was expensively arrayed, and that her mother's dress (for her mother was in the room) and general appearance was by no means humble. There were a number of comely maidens also in attendance, showing little signs of neglect in their attire, and in all respects the household was luxuriously arranged.

'Tell me, Theodote,' said he, 'have you any land of your own?'

'I have not,' she replied.

'Well, then, I suppose your household brings you in a good income.'

'No, I have not a house.'

'Have you a factory, then?'

'No, not a factory either.'

'How then do you get what you need?'

'When I find a friend, and he is kind enough to help me, then my livelihood is assured.'

'By our lady, that is a fine thing to have. A flock of friends is far better than a flock of sheep, or goats, or oxen. But do you leave it to chance whether friends are to wing their way towards you like flies, or do you use some mechanical device?'

'Why, how could I find any device in this matter?'

'Surely, it would be much more appropriate for you than for spiders. You know how they hunt for their living. They weave gossamer webs, I believe, and anything that comes their way they take for food.'

'Do you advise me, then, to weave a hunting net?'

'No, no. You must not suppose that it is such a simple matter to catch that noble animal, a lover. Have you not noticed that even to catch such a humble thing as a hare people use many devices? Knowing that hares are night-feeders, they provide themselves with night-dogs, and use them in the chase. Furthermore, as the creatures run off at daybreak, they get other dogs to scent them out and find which way they go from their feeding ground to their forms. Again, they are swift-footed, so that they can get away in an open race, and a third class of dogs is provided to catch them in their tracks. Lastly, inasmuch as some escape even from the dogs, men set nets in their runs, so that they may fall into the meshes and be caught.'

'But what sort of contrivance should I use in hunting for lovers?'

'A man, of course, to take the place of the dog; some one able to track out and discover wealthy amateurs for you; able also to find ways of getting them into your nets.'

'Nets, forsooth! What sort of nets have I?'

One you have certainly, close enfolding and well constructed, your body. And within your body there is your heart, which teaches you the looks that charm and the words that please. It tells you to welcome true friends with a smile, and to lock out overbearing gallants; when your beloved is sick, to tend him with anxious care; when he is prospering, to share his joy; in fine, to surrender all your soul to a devout lover. I am sure you know full well how to love. Love needs a tender heart as well as soft arms. I am sure, too, that you convince your lovers of your affection not by mere phrases, but by acts of love.'

'Nay, nay, I do not use any artificial devices.'

'Well, it makes a great difference if you approach a man in the natural and proper way. You will not catch or keep a lover by force. He is a creature who can only be captured and kept constant by kindness and pleasure.'

'That is true.'

'You should only ask then of your well-wishers such services as will cost them little to render, and you should requite them with favours of the same sort. Thereby you will secure their fervent and constant love, and they will be your benefactors indeed. You will charm them most if you never surrender except when they are sharp set. You have noticed that the daintiest fare, if served before a man wants it, is apt to seem insipid; while, if he is already sated, it even produces a feeling of nausea. Create a feeling of hunger before you serve your banquet; then even humble food will appear sweet.'

'How can I create this hunger in my friends?'

'First, never serve them when they are sated. Never suggest it even. Wait until the feeling of repletion has quite disappeared and they begin again to be sharp set. Even then at first let your suggestions be only of most modest conversation. Seem not to wish to yield Fly from them—and fly again; until they feel the pinch of hunger. That is your moment. The gift is the same as when a man desired it not; but wondrous different now its value.'

Theodotë: 'Why do you not join me in the hunt, and help me to catch lovers?'

'I will, certainly,' said he, 'if you can persuade me to come.'

'Nay, how can I do that?'

'You must look yourself, and find a way if you want me.'

'Come to my house then, often.'

Then Socrates, jesting at his own indifference to business, replied:

'It is no easy matter for me to take a holiday. I am always kept busy by my private and public work. Moreover, I have my lady friends, who will never let me leave them night or day. They would always be having me teach them love-charms and incantations.'

'What, do you know that, too?'

'Why, what else is the reason, think you, that Apollodorus and Antisthenes never leave my side? Why have Cebes and Simmias come all the way from Thebes to stay with me? You may be quite sure that not without love-charms and incantations and magic wheels may this be brought about.'

'Lend me your wheel, then, that I may use it on you.

'Nay, I do not want to be drawn to you. I want you to come to me.'

'Well, I will come. But be sure and be at home.'

'I will be at home to you, unless there be some lady with me who is dearer even than yourself.'

It is a significant incident, charmingly related by Xenophon, but not altogether charming in itself, although the humorous irony of Socrates may hide from careless readers all the darker sides of the picture. But Socrates himself is entirely lovable. There is nothing furtive, nothing patronising in the philosopher's attitude. He behaves to Theodotë as he would behave to every one. He admires her beauty, and, like Goldsmith, recognises that a beautiful woman is a benefactress to mankind. But while he knows the strength of her position, he realises its weakness also, and there is a shade of pity in his admiration.

A similar appreciation of women is shown in many passages of the *Symposium*; for example, when Socrates says, 'Women need no perfume: they are compounds themselves of fragrance.' There is that Socratic paradox, also, after the dancing-girl's performance:

> 'This is one proof, among very many, that woman's nature is in no way inferior to man's: she has no lack either of judgment or physical strength.'

He continues his argument by advising his friends to *teach* their wives; and he deals with the weakest point in woman's life—the ignorance in which they were kept. 'Do not be afraid,' he says; 'teach her all that you would wish your companion to know.'

Thereupon Anthisthenes puts the pertinent question: 'If that is your idea, Socrates, why do you not try and train Xanthippë, who is, I believe, the most difficult of all wives, present, past, and future?' To this he gets the following reply:

> 'I have noticed,' says Socrates, 'that people who wish to become good horsemen get a spirited horse, not a tame, docile animal. They think that if they can manage a fiery steed they will find no difficulty with an ordinary horse. My case is the same. I wanted to be a citizen of the world and to mix with all men.

So I took her. I am quite sure that if I can endure her, I shall find no difficulty in ordinary company.'

Thus Socrates draws benefit even from a shrewish wife. His ideas of a happy marriage, and the best means of securing that happiness, are set out for us by Xenophon in the *Œconomicus*. Ischomachus, Socrates' interlocutor, is for all practical purposes Xenophon himself, and the whole passage should be compared with those delightful stories of conjugal happiness—the tale of Panthea, and the wife of Tigranes—which the historian gives us in the Education of Cyrus. The dialogue begins by Socrates asking Ischomachus how he won his sobriquet of 'honest gentleman'—surely not by staying at home!

'No,' replies Ischomachus, 'I do not spend my days indoors: my wife is quite capable of managing our household without my help.'

'Ah, that is what I want to know. Did you train your wife yourself to be all that a wife should be? Or, when you took her from her parents, did she possess enough knowledge to perform her share of house management?'

'Possess knowledge when I took her? Why, she was not fifteen years old, and until then she had lived under careful surveillance—to see and hear, and ask as little as possible. All that she knew was how to take wool and turn it into a dress. All that she had seen was how the spinning-women have their daily tasks assigned. As regards control of appetite, she had certainly received a sound education, and that, I think, is all-important.'

Ischomachus then proceeds to detail his system of education. It begins with husband and wife offering sacrifice together and praying that fortune may aid in teaching and learning what is best for both. Then, as soon as the wife 'is tamed to the hand, and not too frightened to take part in conversation,' the husband explains that they are now partners together, at present in the house, in future in any children that may be born to them. They have each contributed a portion to the common stock, and must now work together in protecting their joint interests. The wife agrees to this, but doubts her own capacity. 'Everything depends on you,' she says; 'my business, mother said, was to be modest and temperate.' The husband then explains the true functions of man and woman and their points of difference. Man has a greater capacity than woman for enduring heat and cold, wayfaring and route-marching. God meant for him outdoor work. Woman has less capacity for bearing fatigue; she is more affectionate, more timorous. God has imposed upon her the indoor work. Finally, to men and women alike in equal measure, God gives memory, carefulness, and self-control. Custom agrees with the divine ordinance. For a woman to stay quiet at home, instead of roaming abroad, is no disgrace: for a man to remain indoors is discreditable. The wife is like the queen bee, on whom all the work of the hive depends; and a good mistress soon wins the loyal love of all her servants. So the conversation proceeds, and with this beautiful sentence the first conjugal lesson ends:

> 'But your sweetest joy will be to show yourself my superior, and to make me your servant; then you need not fear that as the years roll on you will lose your place of honour in the house; you will be sure that, though you are no longer young, your honour will increase; even as you become a better partner to myself and the children, and a better guardian of the home; for it is not beauty, but virtue, that nurtures the growth of a good name.'

But Ischomachus does not confine his teaching to words. He explains to Socrates how once he asked his wife for some household article which she could not find, and how deeply she blushed at her heedless ignorance. So he gives her a practical lesson in household management by taking her over the house and explaining the uses of the various rooms and different utensils, expatiating the while on the beauty of order—'for a beauty like the cadence of sweet music dwells even in pots and pans set out in neat array.' His wife profits by the lesson, and henceforth everything is in its proper place.

He deals faithfully, too, with that most pardonable of woman's weaknesses, the desire to please, that leads some ladies to attempt to improve upon nature. So when one day he finds his wife with powder and rouge upon her cheeks, and wearing high-heeled shoes, he begins like this :

> ' Dear wife, would you think me a good partner in our business if I were to make a display of unreal wealth, false money, and sham purples, wood coated with gold ? '
>
> ' Nay, surely not,' she replies.
>
> ' And as regards my body, would you hold me as more lovable if I were to anoint myself with pigments and paint my eyes ? '
>
> ' Nay, I would rather look into your eyes and see them bright with health.'
>
> ' Believe me, then, dear wife, I am not better pleased with this white powder and red paint than I should be with your natural hue.'

So after that day the young wife gives up cosmetics, and on her husband's advice takes healthy exercise instead ; the physical training he recommends being ' to knead the dough and roll the paste ; to shake the coverlets and make the beds.'

With one last anecdote we must end. Socrates asks his friend whether beside his practical wisdom he has any rhetorical and judicial skill.

> ' Of course I have,' says Ischomachus. ' I am always hearing and debating cases in my own household. Yes, and before to-day I have been taken on one side, and have had to stand my trial, to see what punishment I should bear and what fine I should pay.'
>
> ' And how do you get on ? ' says Socrates.
>
> ' When I have the advantage of truth on my side,

well enough ; but when I have not truth with me I can never make the worse cause appear the better.'

'And how is that ? Who is the judge ? '

'*My wife.*'

Ischomachus' home, at least, is no doll's-house. His wife is as far removed from the humble drudge with whom the ordinary Athenian was familiar as she is from the painted odalisque who to the Ionian was the ideal of the perfect woman.

X.—Aristophanes

The work of Aristophanes is a pendant to that of Euripides, and is often inspired by a much more serious purpose than is commonly supposed. Aristophanes is no mere vulgar buffoon, and most of his obscenity is an empty parade made necessary by the conditions of the Attic stage which Aristophanes himself in the course of his career rendered obsolete. He was a member of the Socratic Circle (the famous Symposium ends with Socrates expounding to Agathon and Aristophanes the nature of tragedy and comedy, and explaining the essential similarity of their functions), and in his early manhood he fell under the spell of the great tragedian. Of all his comedies there is hardly one which in language, music, and dramatic technique does not reveal the intimate harmony that exists between the two men. Aristophanes and Euripides, like our Shelley, were born to be lyric poets, and they both possess the divine gift of melody. But they were interested in so many other things, in politics, in feminism, and in social reform, that art with them often takes the second place. As men they are incomparably greater than such self-centred poets as Sophocles; as artists they neither aim at nor achieve his academic perfection. Their methods are curiously alike, and it is because Aristophanes knows Euripides so well, and is in such intimate sympathy with him, that the constant parody of the Euripidean style in the comedies never becomes wearisome.

Parody, gross humour, indecency even, these were the qualities that a comic poet at Athens had necessarily to display, and Aristophanes, having chosen his medium of expression, is compelled to obey the restrictions of the comic stage. Moreover, it is obvious that he enjoys indulging his humour to the utmost. The wit of Euripides is restrained and ironical, with something of the bitterness of old age; Aristophanes in most of his plays has the exuberance of youthful spirits and an overflowing stock of fantastic inventions.

But a dramatist, even a comic dramatist, however fantastic and inventive his humour may be, must have some foundation of serious purpose, and that foundation Aristophanes takes very largely from Euripides. His three chief themes are the same as those of the tragedian: firstly, that war is a curse—it is useful perhaps for politicians and soldiers, but only brings disaster to real workers; secondly, that a belief in gods made in mortal shape is absurd—such a belief will certainly lead to farcical situations, which if treated realistically will be excellent material for a comic poet ; thirdly, that women are as capable, intellectually and morally, as men—their experience of house-management especially fits them for carrying on the business of a State, and a feminist administration might solve many problems that have proved too hard for men. The first of these themes appears in the plot of the *Acharnians*, the *Peace*, and the *Knights* ; the second in the *Birds*, the *Frogs*, and the *Plutus* ; the feminist plays are the *Women at the Festival*, the *Lysistrata*, and the *Women in Assembly*.

It is obvious that the treatment of these themes in tragedy and comedy will be different ; but the initial point of view is very much the same. As for the abuse of Euripides, and there is plenty in the comedies, it is merely part of the comic game, and it is foolish to take it seriously. Aristophanes, Euripides, Plato, and Socrates were all close friends, as intimate one with the other as are our leading politicians, and to speak of Aristophanes ' attacking ' Euripides and Socrates is to misread the situation.

It is not to be supposed that all the members of the Socratic Circle thought alike on all subjects, and even as regards feminism there are some points of difference between Euripides and Aristophanes. The comic poet is rather interested in the woman's cause than devoted to it, and in many of his plays he certainly hesitates between the gross realism of the phallic god and the new ideas of feminist doctrine. Often, too, in his theatre women occupy as insignificant a place as they did in the actual life of his time. In the *Wasps*, for example, Philocleon's household apparently consists of his grown-up son and the attendant slaves: nothing is said of wife or daughter. In the *Knights*, ' Demos '—John Bull —has no Mrs. Bull to keep him company: his domestic arrangements are in the hands of men slaves. In the *Clouds* there is a vivid picture of Socrates at home: house, furniture, and pupils are all described, but nothing of Xanthippe. So in the *Acharnians* and the *Peace* we have household scenes, but no women take part in the action: the women are there, but they are persons of no importance. Trygæus, before setting off on his adventurous voyage, bids an affectionate farewell to his little children, but for his wife he has no message. The Megarian sells his two daughters for a handful of leeks and a measure of salt, and then prays to all his saints that he may be lucky enough to get as good a price for his mother and his wife.

A realist, depicting life at Athens in the fifth century, was compelled to give women an insignificant rôle, but even in this group of plays Aristophanes makes one exception, the exception, perhaps, that proves the rule, for even under the harem system the masterful woman will sometimes come to the front, and Haroun al Raschid goes in fear of Zobeida. In the *Clouds*, Strepsiades is married and by no means independent of his wife: the lady is mentioned, although she takes no part in the play, and the reasons of this difference are instructive. Strepsiades himself is a person of inferior social position, lacking both in will-power and intellectual force; his wife is a woman of property, the daughter of a noble family and herself of determined character. Using all these advantages, she is just able to hold her own with her feeble, foolish husband, and to insist at least on a compromise when their opinions differ.

But it is possible to make too much of the absence of women characters, for the conditions of performance at the Lenæan festival were all against feminine interests, and even though the plot of many of the comedies has little to do with women, there are constant flashes that reveal the author's feminist sympathies. Of all the episodes in the *Birds* there is none quite so freshly humorous as the arrest of Iris, the girl messenger of the Gods, and even in the midst of the fierce political raillery of the *Knights* there comes the delicious interlude of the lady triremes meeting in council; the old stager Nauphantë, addressing the assembly first and revealing the goings-on of the Government, followed by the shy young thing 'who has never come near men,' and is determined to keep her independence, 'heaven forfend, no man shall ever be my master.' Indeed, considering the state of Athens and the necessity that lay upon a comic poet of suiting the tastes of his audience, the real surprise is that no less than three of the remaining eleven plays—the *Lysistrata*, the *Women at the Festival*, and the *Women in Assembly*—should be concerned with the feminist movement and be written in open advocacy of the women's cause.

The Women at the Festival—*Thesmophoriazusæ*—is the lightest of the three, and is really a very brilliantly written feminist 'revue.' Euripides is the 'compère,' and in various disguises takes part in most of the incidents. He has heard that the women, now assembled in their own festival to which no men are admitted, intend to have him put to death, firstly for being a playwright and secondly as a slanderer of womenkind. He goes round to his friends to save him (the scene is a parody on the *Alcestis*), and first of all to his fellow-dramatist, Agathon. But Agathon, whose music is then burlesqued, is too much like a woman to be of any assistance. He is another of the inner Socratic Circle, but in the way of jest the most infamous conduct is imputed to him: his appearance is as ambiguous as his morals, and all he can do for

Euripides is to lend him some articles of women's dress for the purpose of a disguise. So Euripides has to fall back on his father-in-law, Mnesilochus, the buffoon of the piece, and there follows one of those scenes of disrobing with which we are familiar on the modern stage. The old gentleman is undressed, shaved all over and arrayed in woman's garments, *i.e.*, he exchanges his rough white blanket for a finer yellow one; winds a band-corset round his breast and puts on a hair-net and bonnet. He is now to all appearances a woman and goes to the Thesmophorian Festival to find out the details of the women's proposal.

The women assemble, and in an elaborate burlesque of a public meeting recount their grievances against Euripides. It is because of the poet that men have become so suspicious: they scent a lover everywhere, spy on their wives, and lock up the store cupboards. Old men who once would take young wives now remain unmarried, for the poet has told them, 'When an old man marries a young wife, the lady is master.' Finally, by his atheistical doctrines, Euripides has ruined many an honest flower-girl, for men do not offer garlands now to the gods. Then Mnesilochus gets up for the defence. 'I detest the fellow as much as you do,' he says; 'but it is unreasonable to be annoyed with him for talking about one or two of our weaknesses—we have ten thousand which he has never mentioned.' He then proceeds to dilate on some of the frailties which Euripides has omitted; but he is stopped by his angry audience. 'There is nothing so bad as a woman who is naturally shameless'—the chorus say—'*except it be a woman.*'

A fierce discussion begins, until their arguments are interrupted by the appearance of Cleisthenes, one of those womanish men so unpleasantly familiar in Athens, who tells the assembly that a real man is among them. Suspicion at once falls on Mnesilochus; he is discovered by plain evidence to be of the male sex, and is seized by the women. He makes a gallant attempt to escape by snatching a baby from a woman's lap, and holding it to ransom (a parody on Euripides' *Telephus*); but, when he unfastens the child's wrappings, it is not a baby, but a leather skin, full of wine, which the lady has brought for her private refreshment during the proceedings. He then decides to send to Euripides for help, and a parody of the *Palamedes* ends the first part of the play.

The intermezzo, as we might call it, between the two acts is a humorous statement of the women's case on strict Euripidean lines:

Each and every one [the chorus sings] abuses the tribe of women: we are everything that is bad. Well, then, *why do you marry us?* Why do you keep us indoors, as though we were something very, very precious? Why, if we peep out of a window, does every man want to get a good view of our face? As a matter of fact, women are better than men, not worse; they are less greedy, less dishonest, less vulgar; lastly, they alone are the *mothers* of heroes.

The second act is a series of attempts by Euripides to rescue his defender. In the first episode the tragedian appears disguised as the Menelaus of his Helen. Old Mnesilochus is the fair but frail queen, and the scene is *supposed* to change to Egypt. But the women refuse to let their captive free, and he is finally handed over to a north-country policeman, an illiterate gentleman with a very strong accent. On him Euripides tries the effect of another tragedy. Disguised as Perseus he insists that Mnesilochus is the captive maiden, Andromeda, and that he has come to release her. But the policeman proves obdurate. Then Euripides plays his last card. Remembering that all policemen have a *faiblesse* for the weaker sex, he disguises himself as an old woman, and comes in, leading by the hand a young and attractive female. The policeman begins at once to soften, and when the plump flute-girl sits down on his knee he capitulates, murmuring, 'What a swaät toöng: it's reaäl Attic hoöney!' A last vestige of professional caution makes him ask the old lady her name. Euripides, having to choose a title, chooses a good one, and says, 'Artemisia,' which the policeman enters as 'Artamouxia' in his note-book, and then, handing over the custody of his prisoner to the old lady he retires indoors with his young aquaintance. The other pair hasten to make their escape, and the play ends with the policeman's despairing cry, Artamouxia, Artamouxia, where are you?'

The *Lysistrata*, 'breaker up of armies,' is a much stronger play, and the heroine is a masterpiece of dramatic characterisation. From the beginning of the action, when she stands in the darkness waiting for the women she has summoned, and frowning with impatience—'although a frown spoils her looks,' as her one companion tells her—until the end, when, her purpose accomplished, she can say, 'Let man stand by woman and woman by man. Good luck to all, and pray God that we make no more of these mistakes,' she is a real living woman. If Aristophanes had written nothing else, *Lysistrata* shows that he understood the female mind almost as well as Euripides himself: better far than most women authors, except only the incomparable Jane, to whose Emma in masterfulness and independence the Athenian lady bears a close resemblance. The plot of the play is simple. Under the lead of Lysistrata the women of Athens make a league with the women of Sparta, Bœotia, Corinth, and the other

Greek States (for the solidarity of women is one of the key-notes of the play), to stop the war. For this purpose they put into effect both active and passive measures: they bind themselves by oath to have no further intercourse with their husbands until peace is made (the women at first object, but under the lead of the athletic Spartan finally agree), and they also seize the Acropolis with the treasury. The old men left at home, and the officials, for most of the men are at the war, try to use force; but Lysistrata has marshalled and drilled her women. In a very vivid scene the men attack, but, 'Up guards, and at them!' cries Lysistrata; and the forces of male law and order, as represented by the Scythian policemen, are put to ignominious flight. Then the men think it expedient to propose a friendly meeting, and the 'conversation' between Lysistrata and the Chief Commissioner is the most instructive part of the play.

'Why have you seized the treasury?' he asks. Lysistrata explains that all wars depend on financial considerations, and that the women mean to stop supplies. His argument, that women have no administrative skill or financial knowledge, is countered by the plain facts of home management. 'It is not the same thing,' says the Commissioner; 'this is a war fund.' Then Lysistrata declares that the war has to stop—now, at once.

In our retiring modesty we have put up long enough with what you men have been doing. You would not let us speak, but we have not been at all satisfied with you. *We* knew what was going on, although we stay indoors. Over and over again we were told of some new big mistake you had made. With pain in our hearts we would put on a smile and ask, 'What have you done to-day about the peace?' 'But—what's that to you?' our man would say. 'Hold your tongue.' And so I did, then (says Lysistrata), but I am not going to now. I have heard the strain quite long enough, 'Men must see to war's alarms.' This is my version of the tune: 'Women shall see to war's alarms'; and if you listen to my advice you will not be troubled by war's alarms any more. All you have to do is to hold your tongue, as we used to do.

At this the Commissioner breaks in furiously: 'You accursed baggage, I hold my tongue before you! Why, you are wearing a veil now to hide your face. May I die rather.' But his anger does him little good.

'If that is your difficulty,' says Lysistrata, 'take my veil'—and she puts it on his head—'and now hold your tongue; moreover, here is my wool-basket, so you may munch beans and card the wool; for now "Women, women never shall be slaves."' And so the scene ends with the triumphant chorus.

Between this, the first act, and the second there is a short interval of time; and when we see Lysistrata again she is having some difficulty in keeping her women together and away from their husbands.

'You long for your men,' she says; don't you think they are longing for you? I am sure they are finding the nights very hard. Hold out, good friends, and bear it for a little while longer.' Her arguments are successful, and soon the first man comes in, with a baby in his arms, prepared to submit to any terms. But till the peace is made, no arrangement is possible and the poor husband goes away unsatisfied. Finally, a joint deputation of Spartans and Athenians appear before Lysistrata. She, as a woman, and therefore, she says, a person of sense, has no difficulty in arranging for them terms of peace which are satisfactory to both sides; and so the play ends with a 'necklace' dance, men and women dancing hand in hand.

But this brief summary gives little idea of all the devices of stage-craft in which the *Lysistrata* abounds. It is eminently an acting play, and can still fill a theatre. The language is certainly gross and its heroine is entirely lacking in modest reticence, but a glance at the French adaptation by M. Donnay, of the Academy, and especially at the additional episodes there introduced, will prove that grossness is not the worst thing in the world, and that a quiet tongue does not always mean a virtuous mind.

The Women in Assembly, *Ecclesiazusæ*, is much less vigorous. Written twenty years later than the *Lysistrata*, it shows plain signs of old age and failing powers. Euripides and Socrates have both passed away; the Socratic Circle has broken up. Tragedy is dead, and comedy is dying, for Aristophanes has lost most of that 'vis comica' which was his most wonderful possession. The influence of Plato is substituted for the influence of Euripides, and the play is a parody of feminist theories as they are developed in the Republic.

The construction, however, is poor: the action halts and changes midway in the play; the first part is effective enough, but it would be more effective if we did not remember the *Lysistrata*, whose themes it repeats with less vigour.

At the beginning of the play Praxagora is waiting in the darkness for the women she has summoned to appear. They have resolved to disguise themselves as men, and to attend the assembly which has been called for that morning. There they are to propose and carry a resolution that the State shall be handed over to the management of women. Presently they begin to assemble; their husbands are safely in bed and asleep, for their wives have taken measures that they should have a restful night. Sticks, cloaks, shoes, and false beards are produced and adjusted, but before they set out to pack the assembly Praxagora proposes a rehearsal of their arguments. The ladies who have confined their attention to *looking* like men prove not very expert at speaking in the male style, and Praxagora herself has to give them a sample speech.

Things go wrong [she says] because we choose our government on wrong principles. It is a government by classes, and every one considers his own personal interests. Public money is paid away for private gain. A government of women would alter all this, for women by experience in house management know how to get full value for money. Secondly, women are conservative, and would never agree to any violent change in the finances or the tariff; they are natural economists, and specious cries of fair trade would have no effect upon them. Thirdly, as war ministers, they are certain to be successful; their experience in providing meals will ensure that the soldiers are well fed, and they are not likely to risk unduly the lives of their own sons. Lastly, women are so used to trickery that it will be very hard to trick them. *Therefore*, without any further talking or inquiry as to what women are likely to do, the best thing is to entrust them with the government.

The women by the end of the speech have learnt their parts, and with one last instruction to thrust their elbows into the face of any policeman who tries to interfere they all set out for the assembly. Then Blepyrus, the elderly husband of Praxagora, appears, and the play begins to deteriorate, for it is one of the most dexterous touches in the *Lysistrata* that the husbands are for the most part away from home, and therefore can take no part in the action. Blepyrus and his neighbours have found that their wives have disappeared together with their cloaks and shoes. While they are standing in doubt they hear strange news. The assembly convened that morning to consider the vital question of State reform is already over; it was so well attended and so punctual to time that many men came too late to vote or to receive their attendance fee. A resolution has been passed unanimously that tailors shall provide clothes and bakers bread, free gratis to all; and, furthermore, that the government shall be in the hands of women. A good-looking young man, who made a most effective speech, was chiefly responsible for this change of policy. He pointed out that women could keep a secret far better than men; that they were in the habit of trusting one another, and that they never would be likely to plot against the government; moreover, everything but woman-government had been tried already without much success, and the experiment was well worth making. Blepyrus and his friends acquiesce in the *fait accompli*, and when Praxagora returns she learns from her husband that women are now in authority. The socialistic State begins at once to take shape. Praxagora decrees a community of property—land, food, slaves, belong now to the State—every one possesses everything. Women are part of the community of goods, but to avoid disputes the less well-favoured women and men are to have the first choice of partners, and such unions are purely temporary.

Law courts, gambling saloons, and night clubs are all summarily closed; for these appurtenances of civilisation are incompatible either with socialism or feminism. The difficulty of work is disposed of by the convenient institution of slavery, and a *régime* of universal happiness and feasting begins.

Thus far the first section of the play. The second part, which is very inferior, attempts to show the working of the new system. Praxagora disappears, and the characters are mere mechanical figures. A man, A; a man, B; a young man; a young woman; three old women. The scenes are coarse and uninteresting, nor is the prosiness of the dialogue relieved by any of the vivid touches of humour which mark the poet's earlier plays. Finally, this section, like the first, ends with a banquet, given by the State, and open to all.

The *Ecclesiazusæ* is plainly inspired by Plato's theories of communism and feminism as we have them now in the *Republic* and the *Laws*. A further example of the connection between the comedian and the philosopher is the Aristophanic tale of the origin of sex in Plato's Symposium. The story—a Platonic myth with a difference—is so good a specimen both of Aristophanes' humour and of the gay fashion in which the Greeks anticipate modern science that it is a pity its length prevents quotation.

In ancient days [according to Aristophanes] there were not two sexes but three, the children of the sun, the earth, and the moon. Men were round in shape, with four feet and hands, two faces, and they were able both to walk and to roll. In the pride of their strength they rebelled against heaven, and Zeus cut them in twain. Apollo was bidden to heal the places, but the two halves pined one for the other, and so in pity the god turned their bodies round, and men became in shape such as we see them now.

There are many other details, but the most striking point in the story is the recognition of the original identity of sex. The man and the woman are not separate and opposite, but rather complementary halves of one organism, which once included both; they are a divided whole, and that is why men and women yearn one for the other. How far the tale is Aristophanes' invention, how far Plato's, cannot be decided, but the doctrine of the identity of sex-qualification is the common possession of all the Socratic Circle, and forms as clearly the basis of Plato's serious philosophy as it does of the humorous apologue of Aristophanes.

XI.—Plato

Plato differs from most of the Socratic Circle in that he is, above all things, a visionary and a theorist. He is essentially a masculine genius (with him we hear nothing of wife and children), and he lacks that grip of reality which the natural feminist, Euripides, instinctively possesses. He regarded the condition of society in his native city with a mixture of dislike and contempt, and he saw that the main cause of this condition was the indifference to women and children which the ordinary Athenian prided himself on displaying. In his feminism and his educational reforms, Plato is deeply influenced by Spartan teaching, but the main structure is his own work, based not on any actual experience, but on ideal theory. In this idealism lies both the strength and weakness of his feminist doctrine. He refuses to allow himself to be influenced, as Aristotle after him was influenced, by the actual state of inferiority to which Athenian women had been reduced; but in forming a society which should be the opposite of the degenerate Athens of his day, he is inclined to disregard some of the invincible facts of human nature.

Plato's feminist doctrines are most clearly stated in the fifth book of the *Republic* and the sixth, seventh, and eighth books of the *Laws*. These works are accessible to English readers (or, rather, their rough substance is accessible, for we can never reproduce the delicate music of Plato's prose, and his subtle irony evaporates in English) in Jowett's translation, and in the excellent version of the *Republic* by Davies and Vaughan. But it may be convenient to give a brief summary of his argument.

In the fifth book of the *Republic* the ideal State is being discussed, and the rule κοινὰ τὰ τῶν φίλων ('among friends everything is common property') has been laid down. It has, moreover, been made applicable to wives and children, for Plato at first hardly escapes from the fallacy that a man's wife is as much a piece of property as a dog or a table. The organization of the communistic *régime* in detail then comes up for consideration, but it is unanimously resolved that the question of community of women is of vital importance and must be explained at once. The philosopher accordingly, with some pretended reluctance, begins with a prayer to Nemesis—'I am on a slippery road, and fear lest missing my footing I drag my friends down with me'—and thus approaches his subject:

'The aim of our theory was, I believe, to make our men, as it were, guardians of a flock?'

'Yes.'

'Let us keep on the same track and give corresponding rules for the propagation of the species, and for rearing the young; and let us observe whether we find them suitable or not.'

'How do you mean?'

'Thus. Do we think that the females of watch-dogs ought to guard the flock along with the males, and hunt with them, and share in all their other duties; or that the females ought to stay at home, because they are disabled by having to breed and rear the cubs, while the males are to labour and be charged with all the care of the flocks?'

'We expect them to share in whatever is to be done; only we treat the females as the weaker, and the males as the stronger.'

'Is it possible to use animals for the same work if you do not give them the same training and education?'

'It is not.'

'If, then, we are to employ the women in the same duties as the men, we must give them the same instructions?'

'Yes.'

'To the men we give music and gymnastic.'

'Yes.'

'Then we must train the women also in the same two arts, giving them, besides, a military education and treating them in the same way as the men.'

The professional humorist is then requested to refrain from the obvious jokes suggested by the idea of women stripped for exercise or old ladies practising athletics, and to remember that all such things are purely matters of custom. The real question is whether the nature of the human female is such as to enable her to share in all the employments of the male, or whether she is wholly unequal to any, or equal to some and not to others; and, if so, to which class military service belongs. Women certainly are different from men, but we must not be misled by the word 'different.' A bald-headed man is different from a long-haired man, but he may be just as good a cobbler, or a statesman. So women differ from men in the part they play in the propagation of the species; but that difference does not affect the question as to whether men and women should engage in the same pursuits. The argument of the adaptability of the sexes to various occupations is discussed, and this point is reached:

'I conclude then, my friend, that none of the occupations which comprehend the ordering of a State belong to woman as woman, nor yet to man as man; but natural gifts are to be found here and there in both sexes alike; and, so far as her nature is concerned, the woman is admissible to all pursuits as well as the man: though in all of them the woman is weaker than the man.'

'Precisely so.'

'Shall we, then, appropriate all virtues to men and none to women?'

'How can we?'

'On the contrary, we shall hold, I imagine, that one woman may have talents for medicine, and another be without them; and that one may be musical and another unmusical?'

'Undoubtedly.'

'And shall we not also say, that one woman may have qualifications for gymnastic exercises and for war, and another be unwarlike and without a taste for gymnastics?'

'I think we shall.'

'Again, may there not be a love of knowledge in one, and a distaste for it in another? And may not one be spirited, and another spiritless?'

'True again.'

'If that be so, there are some women who are fit, and others who are unfit, for the office of guardians. For were not those the qualities we selected, in the case of men, as marking their fitness for that office?'

'Yes, they were.'

'Then, as far as the guardianship of a state is concerned, there is no difference between the natures of the man and of the woman, but only various degrees of weakness and strength?'

'Apparently there is none.'

'Then we shall have to select duly qualified women also to share in the life and official labours of the duly qualified men; since we find that they are competent to the work, and of kindred nature with the men.'

It seems to Plato that it is both practicable and desirable that men and women should have the same training and the same duties; not, indeed, all men and all women, for Plato's is an aristocratic State and he is chiefly legislating for his guardian class, but at least the better men and the better women. So he does not shrink from absolute similarity of education :

> Then the wives of our guardians must strip for their exercises, inasmuch as they will put on virtue instead of raiment, and must bear their part in war and the other duties comprised in the guardianship of the State, and must engage in no other occupations: though of these tasks the lighter parts must be given to the women rather than to the men, in consideration of the weakness of their sex. But as for the man who laughs at the idea of undressed women going through gymnastic exercises, as a means of realising what is most perfect, his ridicule is but ' unripe fruit plucked from the tree of wisdom,' and he knows not, to all appearance, what he is laughing at or what he is doing: for it is, and ever will be, a most excellent maxim, that the useful is noble and the hurtful base.

Thus the first wave of the discussion is successfully surmounted : the second and more dangerous is the proposition that wives and children shall be held in common. The company refuse to admit without discussion that it is either desirable or practicable, and a double line of argument is used. If men and women are educated and live together, human nature will soon bring about even closer associations. Any irregular union would be an offence against the State, and it is of the first importance to science that the best citizens should have the largest number of children. Therefore marriages and births must be a matter of State regulation, and any possible discontent must be averted by an elaborate system of pretence. The details are fixed:

'As fast as the children are born they will be received by officers appointed for the purpose, whether men or women, or both: for I presume that the State offices also will be held in common both by men and women.'

'They will.'

'Well, these officers, I suppose, will take the children of good parents and place them in the general nursery under the charge of certain nurses, living apart in a particular quarter of the city; while the issue of inferior parents, and all imperfect children that are born to the others, will be concealed, as is fitting, in some mysterious and unknown hiding-place.'

'Yes, if the breed of the guardians is to be kept pure.'

'And will not these same officers have to superintend the rearing of the children, bringing the mothers to the nursery when their breasts are full, but taking every precaution that no mother shall know her own child, and providing other women that have milk, if the mothers have not enough: and must they not take care to limit the time during which the mothers are to suckle the children, committing the task of sitting up at night, and other troubles incident to infancy, to nurses and attendants?'

'You make child-bearing a very easy business for the wives of the guardians.'

'Yes, and so it ought to be.'

The second argument may be briefly stated. In the ideal State there will be no such thing as private property: a man will not have a house or dogs of his own, *therefore* (for our philosopher again seems hardly to realise that the analogy between house and wife is not quite exact), he will not have a wife and children of his own. The whole subject concludes with a return to the original topic of equality of opportunity in these terms :

'Then you concede the principle that the women are to be put upon the same footing as the men, according to our description, in education, in bearing children, and in watching over the other citizens, and that whether they remain at home or are sent into the field, they are to share the duties of guardianship with the men, and join with them in the chase like dogs, and have everything in common with them so far as it is at all possible, and that in so doing they will be following the most desirable course and not violating the natural relation which ought to govern the mutual fellowship of the sexes ? '

'I do concede all this,' he replied.

'Then does it not remain for us,' I proceeded, 'to determine whether this community can possibly subsist among men as it can among other animals, and what are the conditions of its possibility ? '

'You have anticipated me in a suggestion I was about to make.'

'As for their warlike operations, I suppose it is easy to see how they will be conducted.'

'How ? ' he asked.

'Why, both sexes will take the field together and they will also carry with them such of their children as are strong enough, in order that, like the children of all other craftsmen, they may be spectators of those occupations in which, when grown up, they will themselves be engaged : and they will require them, besides looking on, to act as servants and attendants in all the duties of war, and to wait upon their fathers and mothers.'

It will be noticed that Plato does not shrink from the question of military service for women. If a man is unwilling or unable to defend his country, he certainly has no claim to citizen rights, nor has a woman. It may reasonably be argued that the qualification for a vote is neither property nor sex, but the proof that the individual has passed through the period of training necessary to qualify him as a defender of the fatherland. The qualities necessary for a soldier are three: courage, strength, and skill. No one acquainted with women can doubt that they possess the first: in the passive courage which a modern soldier chiefly needs it is possible that women have a slight advantage over men, and they usually recover more quickly from wounds. The strength that is required in modern warfare is chiefly endurance: the power to stand exposure to the weather, insufficient food, lack of sleep and comfort; marching capacity. No one who knows the vagabonds and strollers of our English roads will say that women are not capable of supporting all these hardships as well as men. The female tramp is every whit as sturdy and hardy as her male companion. Finally, the skill to handle a gun and the power of shooting straight are matters almost entirely of training: the natural qualities, a steady hand and a sharp eye, that help such a training are by no means predominantly male characteristics.

Plato for his part is very insistent on this question, and returns to it several times in the *Laws*. The State is to maintain schools, where the art of war in all its branches shall be taught to males and females alike. Gymnastics and horsemanship are as suitable to women as to men. Boys and girls together must learn the use of the bow, the javelin, and the sling, and in every well-ordered community at least one day a month shall be set aside for warlike exercise, in which men, women and children shall take part. Female education will include a definite military training: the girls will learn how to use their weapons and to move about lightly in armour; the grown woman will study evolutions and tactics. Finally, in all public festivals and competitions the unmarried girls shall compete with the youths in running and in contests in armour.

It is on this point of military training, perhaps, that Plato stands apart from modern sentiment: most of his other ideals of feminine education are in process of being realised, even that which allowed the educated woman to become herself a teacher, and rank with male colleagues. In the inner circle of the Academy, the first University College of which we know, men and women met on equal terms, and shared responsiblities and privileges. The names of two such women (neither of them, be it noted, Athenians) are recorded for us by Dicæarchus and Lastheneia of Mantinea and Axiothea of Phlius, 'who even used to wear male attire,' hold out their hands across the centuries to Mrs. Bryant and Miss Busk.

Plato, indeed, in spite of his idealism, is often very practical, and on the question of marriage his doctrine is most sound.

> The simple law of marriage is this: A man *must* marry before he is thirty-five; if not, he shall be fined and lose all his privileges. Mankind are immortal because they leave children behind them; and for a man to deprive himself of immortality is impiety. He who obeys the law shall be free and pay no fine; but the disobedient shall pay a yearly fine, in order that he may not imagine that his celibacy will bring him ease or profit: moreover, he shall not share in any of the honours which the State gives to the aged.

Marriage is to be regarded as a duty, and 'every man shall follow, not after the marriage which is most pleasing to himself, but after that which is most beneficial to the State.' This cannot be effected by definite regulations, but we should 'try and charm the spirits of men into believing' that their children are of more importance than themselves, and that a child's disposition will depend upon the happy blending of its parents.

Plato realises that children are the State's vital

interest, and his concern for them extends to the period before birth. Husband and wife are to consider how they are to produce for the State the best and fairest specimens of children which they can. If proper attention is given to anything, success is certain; and the eugenic system is to be under the definite control of a committee of women, who shall meet every day and spend a third part of the day in ensuring that the regulations for perfect births are duly carried out. Their care is to be expressly extended to the future mothers, for the period of a child's life before birth is equally decisive, and the young wife must be carefully tended, kept from excessive pleasures or pains, and be encouraged to cultivate habits of gentleness, benevolence, and kindness.

Then comes the proper management of infants, and Plato is very convinced of the importance of constant motion for the young child, who in a Greek household was often closely bandaged in swaddling clothes and left to its own resources. He anticipates Aristippus, who, holding that pleasure was the chief end of life, found the best definition of pleasure to be 'a gentle motion,' and he is prepared to make his ideal state for infants at least a pleasant one.

The first principle in relation both to the body and soul of very young children is that nursing and moving about by day and night is good for them all, and that the younger they are the more they will need it. Infants should live, if it were possible, as if they were always rocking at sea. Exercise and motion in the earliest years greatly contribute to create a part of virtue in the soul: the child's virtue is cheerfulness, and good nursing makes a gentle and a cheerful child.

This first period will last till the age of three, when the child will begin to find out its own natural modes of amusement in company with other children: from three to six, boys and girls should live and play together: after six they should separate, and begin to receive instruction.

On the subject of co-education, which may be regarded as the best practical solution for the cure of sex-ignorance, Plato speaks with a rather uncertain voice. His general theory presupposes an identity of training, and the free mingling of boys and girls, young men and women, in sport and work. But he is disturbed by his conviction of the natural badness of boys contrasted with girls:

> Of all animals, the boy is the most unmanageable, inasmuch as he has the fountain of reason in him not yet regulated; he is the most insidious, sharp-witted, and insubordinate of creatures; therefore he must be bound with many bridles.

The further difficulty, that constant friendly intercourse between young men and women may lead to undesirable results is discussed at some length in the *Laws*, p. 835, and the very sensible conclusion is arrived at that a healthy public opinion will be the first result of these natural conditions of comradeship, and that the general sentiment will be the strongest of checks upon undue licence. The importance of example in education and morals is rightly insisted upon :

> The best way of training the young is to train yourself at the same time : not to admonish them, but to be always carrying out your own admonitions in practice.

Finally, education is of supreme importance to a country :

> The minister of education is the most important officer of State ; of all appointments his is the greatest ; he will rule according to law, must be fifty years old, and have children of his own, both boys and girls by preference, at any rate one or the other.

These are some of the salient points of Plato's teaching, but a careful reading of the *Republic* and the *Laws* will reveal many further issues and many side-lights on the main thesis. Plato does not trouble to be rigorously consistent, and, like Euripides, he does not hesitate at times to play the part of the candid friend, and to point out what he thinks are the natural weaknesses of the female sex. Sometimes he is right, sometimes he is wrong. 'Women,' he says, 'are too prone to secrecy and stealth ; they are accustomed to creep into dark places and resist being dragged into the light.'

Here Plato seems to hit the truth. If there is one quality—call it virtue or vice, as you will—which is peculiarly a woman's and not a man's characteristic, it is secretiveness. The result of many centuries of self-suppression, it gives a certain aggravating charm to the female mind, and usually does no particular harm. But it is, perhaps, the chief reason of women's comparative failure in literature. Sincerity in writing is the saving grace, and if a book is not frank, it should never be written. Few women authors resemble Sappho, or Jane Austen, or Mme. Colette in contemporary French literature, who, unlike though they are in the circumstances of their lives, do all make a serious attempt at truth. Most women fail in frankness towards themselves and their readers. George Eliot, Ouida, George Sand (to take another typical and strongly differentiated trio) dissemble their facts as much as they dissemble their names. Like ostriches, they hide their faces under a cloud of words.

XII.—The Attic Orators

To turn from Plato's ideal State to the actual condition of woman's life during the fourth century in Athens, as we have it revealed in the pages of the orators, is like passing from a breezy hillsid into a dark, close-shut room. We see the working of the harem system, with all its atmosphere of secrecy and suspicion. The women are closely watched; for it is presumed that they will be unfaithful to their husbands if they can: they live secluded in the women's quarter of the house—the gynæconitis—and for any strange man to enter their rooms is a grave impropriety. In Demosthenes, for example, we find it imputed to Androtion, as a proof of unbearable insolence, that in his capacity of tax-collector he forced his way into the women's apartments, and compelled the master of the house to hide under the bed, putting him thus to shame before his womankind. That a wife should appear publicly with her husband at a dinner party, and take a share in men's pleasures, is equally an offence against morality. Neæra was known to have sat at dinner with her husband and his friends, and this fact, testified by witnesses, is taken as an obvious proof that she was a woman of abandoned character. The sister of Nicodemus, Isæus argues, could not have been legally married, for she was often seen at entertainments with the man she called her husband, and 'wedded wives do not go out to dinner with their husbands, or expect to join in festivities.'

The doctrine that a wife is her husband's property is applied to the fullest extent, and any offence against that property is punished with the utmost rigour of the law. A husband who finds another man in his harem is allowed to put him to death. At Athens there is no pretence of 'the sanctity of marriage': the offence and the punishment is the same whether the intrigue is with the master's wife or with his concubine: each is equally the master's property, to be protected at any cost. It is a more heinous crime to make love to a woman who belongs to another man than to offer her violence; for the offence is viewed solely from the owner's side, and a woman who willingly yields to another is outraging her lawful master's *amour propre* more deeply than if she were taken by force. The lover is put to death; the ravisher pays a fine: the point of view being much the same as used to hold in English law, where the wife-beater was regarded as a less offensive character than the poacher.

But if the husband of an erring wife had the support of the law, however violent his methods of revenge, the case was very different when the woman was the offended party. There is an anecdote in Plutarch's Life of Alcibiades which reveals the attitude of the Athenian lawgivers.

Hipparete made a prudent and affectionate wife;—but at last growing very uneasy at her husband's associating with such a number of courtesans, both strangers and Athenians, she quitted his house and went to her brother's. Alcibiades went on with his debaucheries, and gave himself no pain about his wife; but it was necessary for her, in order to obtain a legal separation, to give in a bill of divorce to the archon, and to appear personally with it; for the sending of it by another hand would not do. When she came to do this according to law, Alcibiades rushed in, caught her in his arms, and carried her through the market-place to his own house, no one presuming to oppose him, or to take her from him. From that time she remained with him until her death, which happened not long after, when Alcibiades was upon his voyage to Ephesus. Nor does the violence used in this case seem to be contrary to the laws either of society in general or of that republic in particular. For the law of Athens, in requiring her who wants to be divorced to appear publicly in person, probably intended to give the husband an opportunity to meet with her and to recover her.

Plutarch, 'Alcibiades,' Langhorne's Translation.

A wife seeking to escape from an unworthy husband, we see, is regarded in the same light as a slave seeking to escape from his owner, and all the resources of the law are put at the disposal of the husband and the master. There was a constant tendency to think of women and slaves together; and the institution of slavery was certainly one of the most powerful agents in the degradation of women at Athens. A slave-girl was, in the eye of the law, a thing—not a human being, and she was free from all restraints of moral sanction. She was the property of her owner, and her only duty was to obey him in all things: virtue, chastity, modesty, were for her things impossible of attainment; and over the whole business was cast the protection and encouragement of the law. There came into existence a class of women condemned to physical and moral degradation—a class whose very existence was an insult to womankind; so that Aristophanes, at least, has the wit to see that the establishment of a female government would have as one of its first results the forcible abolition of all such recognised and legal forms of vice.

Women and slaves then were linked together; and it must be remembered, as Professor Murray says, that people do not become slaves by a legal process; they become slaves when they are brought into contact with superiors who have the power and the will to use them as tools. There are three principal tests of slavery, ancient or modern, and in ancient life they will often apply equally well to women.

Firstly, slaves are a degraded and immoral class. This was continually insisted upon; and doubtless one result was to produce, in a certain degree, the vices falsely imputed to nature.

Secondly, their work is despised, as unworthy of free men. The harder work was left in the hands of slaves or women, who did not receive any pay, and the super-abundant leisure of the male citizen was devoted to the political life.

Thirdly, the condition of dependence, once fully established, soon produces a feeling of despair. The willingness to die, which is so noticeable in Euripides' heroines, is one of the sure signs of slavery. Slaves are lacking in spirit; some, indeed, are so completely lacking that they are happy in servitude: the impetus to revolt must come from without, especially when the servile state has existed for many centuries.

Slavery may be defined as the economic exploitation of the weaker; and, though it does not exist in our time and land, it offers such a convenient basis for civilisation that various devices are used even now to take its place. There is the theory, for example, that some kinds of work are *higher* than others, and therefore should be paid on a higher scale. Or again, that the same work, if performed by different persons, requires different remuneration.

Many estimates of women's inferiority have ultimately an economic basis. The more lucrative trades and professions are those for which it is considered that women are temperamentally unfit.

It is a noticeable fact that all these general conceptions of women's weakness have always been closely connected with their legal status. In Athens, where women could not hold property, and an heiress was taken over by the nearest male relative as a necessary encumbrance on the estate, the estimate of woman's character was very low. In Alexandria and at Rome, where women by various devices outwitted the law and became possessed of some degree of economic independence, their moral position also changed for the better. In England feminism begins with the Married Women's Property Act.

But as long as slavery, social or economic, is not recognised by the law, it cannot be the curse that it was to ancient life. In Athens it was a legal institution, owing its validity to much the same mode of thought as made the wife also her husband's chattel. It is the business of lawyers to defend the law, and, if the law is bad, their moral sense is necessarily warped in the process; so that it is not surprising if the private speeches of the Attic orators, although they exhibit the natural subtlety of the Athenians in a striking light, by no means give an equally strong impression of moral rectitude. All the orators are the same in this respect. Demosthenes in matters of State was a high-minded patriot; as a lawyer he is, like the rest of his colleagues, a professional liar, and does not scruple to falsify and misrepresent the truth. Lysias so forgets the man in the advocate that he seems to reserve his highest powers for his worst cases, and obviously delights in such a client as the shameless old cripple for whom he writes his most ingenious speech. Isæus has no regard for veracity, and it has been found by painful experience that his unsupported statements, even on simple questions of fact, are, to put it mildly, extremely unreliable. As for Hyperides, he is careless of shame so long as he wins his case; and his gesture, as he bids his fair client display her charms, is like the calculated boldness of the slave-dealer offering his girls to the highest bidder.

But if the orators give us an impression of cunning subtlety which far transcends the bounds that we even now allow to lawyers, their clients are in no better case. By the middle of the fourth century Athens was in full decadence. Her men had lost all the vigour and courage that brought their country safe through the dangers of the Persian Wars: her women, perhaps, were even worse than the men—*corruptio optimi pessima*—and had sunk into a state of utter degradation.

Impotent old men and designing young women are the chief figures in most of Isæus' speeches; and, as his editor says, to have any confidence in the veracity or virtue of his clients argues a truly Arcadian simplicity. There is the case of Euctemon, for example—the old man who divorces his wife and leaves his children, to live with his slave-woman, Alce. This unfortunate, whose youth has been degraded for her master's profit, has her revenge when the old man grows senile. She induces him to remove her from the den of infamy which has been one of the sources of his wealth, to live with her in the drinking-shop over which she is put in charge, and finally to recognise one of her bastards as his own son. The family, threatened by a second marriage, reluctantly consent to help in an adoption which ran counter to the first principles of Attic law; and it is not until the old man's death, when his property falls into dispute, that his 'misfortunes' with the woman (so the advocate euphemistically describes them) come to light. The facts of the case are utterly sordid; but every detail is enveloped by Isæus in a cloud of sophistical arguments which show both a complete absence of moral sense in the advocate and so great a faculty of deception that modern writers have inferred—it need not be said with how little reason—that polygamy was not illegal at Athens, that concubinage was recognised by law, and that bastards had the rights of legitimate children. All three statements are untrue; but they may fairly be deduced from the ever-shifting arguments that the lawyer uses. In another of his cases it is an old man at death's door who marries a young girl, and the usual imputations upon the bride's motives form one of his strongest arguments. In a third, the estate of Pyrrhus, a woman of notoriously bad life is foisted by her brother upon one of her old lovers, and the claim is then made that she is his legal wife.

But to go through the details of Isæus' cases would be merely tedious. In all of them we see that moral degradation and absence of social rectitude which was the natural result of the inferiority of women in the eyes of the Attic law. Women, like children, cannot legally enter into a contract, even if it is only to purchase a bushel of corn; the son of a brother has a stronger claim to an intestate property than the son of a daughter, for the law says, 'males must prevail'; a daughter cannot inherit in her own person; she is only an intermediary by whom the estate is transmitted through marriage to a male of the same blood as her father. A woman's disabilities are painfully plain in Isæus: as for her legal rights, it is hard to discover from his speeches how far they have any actual existence. The orator, at least, when his male clients seem to have the law against them, does not hesitate to appeal to the natural sympathies of the male jurymen; and in the tenth oration we see how shamefully an heiress, in spite of the law's formal protection, could be despoiled by her guardian and her brother.

It is generally assumed that this male superiority before the law had a religious sanction, the necessity of keeping up the family worship, which could only be done by a man. If we were speaking of a primitive society the argument would have some force, but the Athenians of the fourth century were at the end rather than the beginning of their national life: religion was dead, and the foundations of morality undermined; only the law remained unaltered, that women were the inferior sex. How far women contributed themselves to their degradation may be studied in all the orators' speeches, but two cases are especially significant: Antiphon's murder speech 'Against the stepmother,' and Lysias' 'Defence for the murder of Eratosthenes.'

The first is grimly horrible in its sordid realism; as Antiphon says, it is the story of Clytemnestra repeated, but divested now of all its tragic romance. Two women are the chief characters: one a free-born Athenian, the wife of the murdered man; the other a slave, the mistress of the man's friend, one Philoneos. The facts are these: Philoneos gets tired of his mistress' devotion, and determines to rid himself of her by the simple process of selling her into a life of utter degradation. He reveals his intention to his friend, and the two men decide to have one last carouse, the girl waiting upon them, before she goes to her ruin. But the man's wife, who has found her husband as false to her as Philoneos is to his lover, intervenes. She makes the acquaintance of the slave-girl, who is still passionately devoted to her worthless master, and persuades her to regain his affection by a love-potion which she will provide. The girl agrees, and when the two men meet at dinner she pours the potion (which, unknown to her, is a deadly poison) into their cups, giving the larger share to her own false lord. Philoneos falls dead immediately; the other man collapses, and dies some days afterwards. The slave-girl is taken and broken on the wheel; the wife is in this speech accused by her stepson of her share in the crime.

Antiphon's pleadings throw a lurid light on the relations between men and women in a slave State; the speech of Lysias in defence of Eratosthenes' murder is an even more invaluable document. The orator's client is accused of murder, and relies for his defence on the plea that his victim was taken in adultery, and therefore lawfully put to death. The law, at Athens a written, not an unwritten code, is definitely on the accused man's side; but it is curious that this is the only surviving speech in which it is pleaded as an excuse. It seems, indeed, that even the Athenians hesitated to use the ferocious power that the law gave them; and we may imagine, if we will, that this was a test case, brought, perhaps, by one of the Socratic circle, to try the validity of the law in the face of the new feminist doctrines. In any event, the Ionian Lysias, whose honeyed pen was at the service of the highest bidder, was a person thoroughly distasteful to Plato and his friends, and it is probable that in this speech he had the satisfaction both of defending the established order of social morality, and also of striking a shrewd blow at his personal enemies. The speech, which is a model of art, begins with some compliments to the jury, and then Lysias, very ingeniously, makes his client tell the simple story of his life.

> When I decided to marry, gentlemen, and brought a wife into my house, I made this my rule of behaviour. I did not annoy her with excessive vigilance, but on the other hand, I did not leave her too much her own mistress to do whatever she pleased. I kept as close a guard over her as was possible, and took all reasonable care.

(This to conciliate the jury and to show that the damage done was not due to any lack of precautions on the owner's side.)

> After a time a child was born and then I began to feel confidence, and handed over to her the charge of all my goods, thinking that this was the surest bond of union between us. At first, gentlemen, she was the

best of women, a clever housewife and a thrifty, exact in all her management. Then my mother died, and her death has been the cause of all my troubles. My wife went to her funeral; that fellow saw her walking in the funeral procession, and after a time succeeded in corrupting her.

(The jury are meant to draw the inference that women should never leave the house: one appearance in public may mean ruin.)

He watched my wife's maid who goes to do the marketing, made a proposal to her, and soon effected his purpose of seduction. I must tell you, gentlemen, that my humble home is built in two storeys, the upper part similar in style to the ground floor, one containing the women's apartments, the other the men's rooms. Now when our baby was born, the mother began by nursing it herself, and to avoid any risk of her coming down stairs at bath-time, I took up my quarters in the upper rooms, and the women came down to the ground floor. Moreover, we soon got into the way of my wife leaving me to go and sleep with the baby downstairs, so that she might give him the breast and prevent him crying.

(It is, of course, essential that the master's rest at night should not be disturbed, and the jury will agree that this was a legitimate reason for a wife's absence from her proper place.)

This went on for a long time and I never suspected anything. Such an arrant simpleton was I that I thought *my* wife the most virtuous woman in Athens. Well, gentlemen, time passed away, and one day I came back home unexpectedly from the country,

After dinner the baby began to cry and make itself unpleasant: the maid was hurting it on purpose to cause a disturbance, as I heard afterwards, for the fellow was in the house. I told my wife to go and give it the breast to stop it crying, but at first she would not go: she pretended that she was so delighted to see me after my long absence. Finally, when I began to get angry and bade her be off, 'Oh, yes,' she said, 'you want to stay here and make love to the parlourmaid; I caught you pulling her about the other day when you were drunk.' At that I smiled, and she got up and went away, pulling the door to in pretended jest, and taking away the key. I did not think anything of it, nor had I any suspicions: indeed, I soon fell asleep, for I had just come from the country and was glad to get rest. It was getting on for daybreak when she returned and opened the door. I asked her then why the doors had been banging in the night, and she pretended that the child's lamp had blown out, and she had gone next door to get a light. I said nothing and believed her tale. I did, however, notice that her face was covered with powder—although her brother had not been dead a month—but still I said nothing about her conduct. I went out and left the house in silence.

(White cheeks were highly esteemed at Athens, and when a lady wished to be especially attractive, she procured them artificially. In this case the husband is distracted by a double feeling: gratification at his wife's apparent desire to please him, and disgust at her obvious disrespect for a male relative.)

Some time elapsed after these events, gentlemen, and I had no inkling of my misfortune, when one day an old person came up to me. She was sent, as I heard afterwards, by another woman that fellow had seduced and then abandoned, who, in her rage and indignation had spied on him until she found out the reason of his desertion. Well, the old lady came to me near my house, where she was watching, and ' Euphiletus,' said she, ' don't think that I have come in any spirit of officious interference: the man who is wronging you and your wife, as it happens, is an enemy of mine. If you take the maid who goes to market and does your errands, and torture her, you will find out everything. The man is Eratosthenes, of Oea: he is responsible for this; he has seduced your wife and many other women besides: that is his trade.

So the warning comes, and then events move quickly. The husband takes the servant, and by a mixture of promises and threats compels her not only to confess, but to betray her mistress. When next the lover comes to the house—it is alleged by the prosecution that he is beguiled there by the husband, and although this is denied, it is regarded as a quite legitimate plot—the maid informs her master; witnesses are hastily summoned; the door, left unfastened by the girl, is pushed open and the guilty pair are discovered together. Eratosthenes is struck down, his arms are pinioned, and then in the name of the law and in cold blood he is killed. The scene is like the last act of *Scheherazade* without its barbaric magnificence. Of the woman nothing is said, and the speaker concludes by reminding his judges that his cause is theirs, and that the only way to prevent illicit love is to take summary vengeance on the lover.

The point of view, it will be noticed, as regards the marriage relationship, is very different from that expressed by Plato or Aristotle. Plato regards marriage as a temporary connection dictated by mutual interest and dissolvable at will. Aristotle says (*Politics*, 7, 16) :

> As to adultery, let it be held disgraceful for any man or woman to be unfaithful when they are man and wife. If during the time of bearing children anything of the sort occur, let the guilty person be punished with a loss of privileges in proportion to the offence.

The philosophers see that marital fidelity is important chiefly in relation to children and the State, and they attach the same stigma to either of the parties who break the contract. Lysias, as a lawyer, suiting his arguments to a male audience, takes much lower ground. The husband smiles at his own infidelities, but claims the right to commit murder when his wife retaliates.

The *Eratosthenes* is, perhaps, the most vivid picture we have of home-life in Athens, but the general impression given by all the orators is much the same. Women are either cowed into hopeless submission or else they are shamelessly profligate. The occasional exceptions, such as we find in Lysias' speech 'Against Diogiton,' where a widow defends her children's interests with skill and vigour, show that the fault was due to the marriage system rather than to woman's nature. Most of the women, however, are incapable of energy: their prison life has deprived them of the power and will to act. In Lysias' speech 'Against Simon,' for example, the speaker, a bachelor living in an abominable relationship, has his sister and nieces as inmates of his house, and he says: 'These ladies' life has been so decent and orderly that they are ashamed even for the men of their own household to set eyes upon them.' In Demosthenes' speech 'Against Conon,' his unfortunate client, again a bachelor, has his mother keeping house for him. When, after his encounter with the 'Fighting Cocks' Club' he is carried home, his cloak stolen, his lip split, and both eyes closed, the ladies of his establishment, his mother and his female attendants, begin to weep and wail over his sad condition—but they do nothing else. His male acquaintances carry him off to the public bath, there fetch a doctor, and finally remove him to the house of a friend. Even as ministering angels the Athenian women seem to have been ineffective. Only in the case of the imprisonment or the death of their male relatives do they come actively forward, and the business of mourning and funeral lamentation was by convention left almost entirely in their hands.

Most of the Athenian women then, as we see them in the writings of the orators, are mere passive animals; a few, and by no means the least successful, are open in their profligacy. Such an one is the mother of Æschines, as we have her described by Demosthenes in the speech 'On the Crown'; such also the abominable pair, mother and daughter, who are the chief characters in the speech 'Against Neæra,' which is attributed to Demosthenes. Here the mother, Neæra, a woman of notoriously bad character, succeeds in marrying an Athenian citizen, and her daughter Phanô, a person as vicious as herself, by one of those strange turns of fortune only possible in a real democracy, becomes the wife of the King-Archon, the head of the State religion, as we might say, wife of the Archbishop of Canterbury. Such another, finally, is the fair Antigona in Hyperides' speech 'Against Athenogenas,' a lady who combined the professions of broker and courtesan, and was equally successful in both.

Of women who were both virtuous and capable the orators tell us singularly little, and the probable reason is that such women in Athens had almost ceased to exist. Demosthenes and his contemporaries represent the last stage, when their country was already on the brink of political extinction, and the men of Athens had no ideals or examples of womanly virtue to encourage them in their vain struggle against the great military power of the North. The lack of good women was a fatal disaster, but it was a disaster which the Athenians had brought upon themselves, and it led them straight to ruin.

XIII. Aristotle

As the political life of Athens ends with Demosthenes, so the creative force of the Greek genius ceases with Aristotle. There are some brilliant and many charming writers after his time, but they rely for all the originality of their thought on their great predecessors. Aristotle is the last of the creators: '*tout le reste, c'est littérature.*'

Hence his unique importance in the history of human thought: not merely is he, perhaps, the greatest mind that Greece produced, but he has the advantage of coming last in the long line of thinkers on whom nearly all our intellectual life even now depends. In every department of civilised existence the influence of Aristotle must still be taken into account, and his judgment of women's position in society—a view sincerely held and on the whole most temperately expressed—has had far more effect on the world than have the idealist theories of Plato. His statement of the moral disabilities of women is to be found best in the *Ethics*; of their social disabilities in the treatise *On Generation*. The following quotations are from the English translations of those works by Welldon, Jowett, and Platt.

To begin with the moral situation in the *Ethics*. Aristotle several times repeats the statement, common enough in ancient literature, though it seems now open to serious objection, that women are less temperate and continent in their desires than men. He does not blame them, but rather regards them with pity, 'for a woman is naturally in such matters weaker than a man: a man's love is passionate and open; women feel desire and are cunning.'* A line from *The Beguiling of Zeus* is quoted to support this view by the authority of Homer, and the philosopher himself agrees with the common Greek view that for a woman to wish to keep her husband to herself was a proof that she was both unreasonable and lascivious. So, in discussing certain morbid habits, such as the practice of biting one's nails or eating cinders, Aristotle has the significant remark: 'Now whenever nature is the cause of these habits nobody would call people who give way to them incontinent, any more than we should call women incontinent from being not males but females.'† It is, perhaps, this belief in the natural incapacity of women for virtue that is the cause of the depreciatory remarks concerning the essential excellence of an Athenian woman, 'bashful modesty.'

* *Ethics*, vii. 7. † *Ibid*. vii. 6.

It would not be right to speak of a sense of shame as a virtue, for it is more like an emotion than a moral state: at least it may be defined as a kind of fear of ignominy, and in its effects it is analogous to the fear of dangers, for people blush when they are ashamed and turn pale when they are afraid of death. It is clear, then, that both affections are in a sense corporeal, and this seems to be the mark of an emotion rather than a moral state.*

Other slighter defects in the female character, as conceived by Aristotle, are hinted at in the remark: 'It is only exceedingly slavish people who eat and drink beyond the point of surfeit'; and in the well-known description of the 'Magnanimous Man,' Aristotle's ideal, who, unlike the shrill-voiced woman,

will have a deep voice and a sedate manner of speaking and be slow in his movements: he will not be in a hurry or emphatic in speech, for there are not many things he cares for, nor does he regard anything as very important, and these are the causes which make people speak in shrill tones and use rapid movements.†

These are some of the deficiencies in women: we have to go to the *Rhetoric* to get Aristotle's idea of their merits. The passage is significant:

θηλειῶν δὲ ἀρετὴ σώματος μὲν κάλλος καὶ μέγεθος, ψύχης δὲ σωφροσύνη καὶ φιλεργία ἄνευ ἀνελευθερίας.‡

The excellence of females is (*a*) physical, a large and beautiful body; (*b*) mental, virtuous moderation and a love—but not a sordid love—of work.

* *Ethics*, iv. 15 † *Ibid.* iv. 9. ‡ *Rhet.* A. v. 6.

First, it will be seen, comes physical attractiveness. The excellent woman must be good-looking, and by 'good-looking' we mean tall and stout, for ethereal grace does not suit the harem-master's taste. Secondly, she will be temperate in her desires: the word 'Sophrosyne,' 'virtuous moderation,' is the chief virtue in a woman: it is the faculty of 'doing without'—love, food, pleasure, consideration, etc.—and the Greeks, unlike the Romans, really did admire this passive merit even in men. Thirdly comes industry, with the restriction that a woman must not be a slave to work: she has other even more important duties—her master's pleasure, for example—and work must not be allowed to interfere unduly. In his conception of female virtue Aristotle has advanced somewhat from Pericles' negative ideal, but he has not got very far.

The most instructive passages, however, in the *Ethics* are in the Eighth Book, where friendship is considered.

There is another kind of friendship or love depending upon superiority, the friendship or love of a father for a son, of a husband for a wife, of a ruler for a subject. These friendships are of different sorts: the love of a husband for a wife is not the same as that of wife for a husband. There is a different virtue in each, a different function, and different motives. It follows that the services rendered by each party to the other are not the same, nor is it right to expect they should be. In all such friendships as depend upon the principle of superiority, the affection should be proportionate to the superiority; *i.e.*, the better or the more useful party, or whoever may be the superior, should receive more affection than ne gives.

This may sound to us humorous, but Aristotle is quite serious: it is part of his great doctrine of 'proportional equality'; and his only doubt is as to which adjective is most appropriate to man, 'better,' or 'more useful,' or simply 'superior.'* Friendship leads to a discussion of domestic associations, and while the *rule* of a slave-master seems a *right* form of despotism, the association of husband and wife is judged to be 'aristocratical,' for the husband's rule depends upon merit and is confined to its proper sphere. He assigns to the wife all that suitably belongs to her. If the husband is lord of *everything*, he changes the association to an 'oligarchy'; for then he acts unfairly and not in virtue of his superior merit. 'Sometimes the wife rules as being an heiress, but such rule is not based upon merit.'†

Last comes the question of children; and here, at least, we need make no criticisms:

It is evident why mothers love their children more than fathers. The procreation of children is the universal function of animals. In the case of other animals, this is the limit of their association; but men and

* *Ethics*, viii. 8. † *Ibid*, viii. 12.

women unite not only for the procreation of children but for the purposes of life. As soon as they unite, a distribution of functions takes place. Some are proper to the husband and others to the wife; hence they supply one another's needs, each contributing to the common stock. Utility and pleasure seem alike to be found in the marriage relationship, but its basis will be virtue, too. Children are a bond of union, and such marriages as are childless are dissolved with comparatively little difficulty.*

The *Politics* begin with a discussion of slavery, and, by an association of ideas natural in Greek society, for Aristotle never attempts to rise above the conditions of life about him, slaves and women are treated together:

> He who can foresee with his mind is by nature intended to be lord and master; and he who can work with his body is a subject, and by nature a slave: hence, master and slave have the same interest. Nature, however, has distinguished between the female and the slave. For she is not niggardly; she makes each thing for a single use, and every instrument is best made when intended for one and not for many uses. But among barbarians no distinction is made between women and slaves.

It should be noticed here that the essential quality of the master is not physical strength, but mental capacity; it is the mind and not the body that makes the 'natural' slave, the 'live tool,' as Aristotle defines him. Man and woman, master and slave,

* *Ethics*, viii. 8.

these are the foundations of the family. As Hesiod says: ' First a house, then a woman, and then an ox for the plough '; and Aristotle has no difficulty in finding the arrangement right. He puts the question:

> Is there any one intended by nature to be a slave, so that for him the condition of slavery is expedient and right; or, rather, is not all slavery a violation of nature?

And gives the immediate reply:

> There is no difficulty in answering this question on grounds both of reason and of fact. For that some should rule and others be ruled is a thing not only necessary but expedient; from the hour of their birth some are marked out for subjection, others for rule.

The law, he thinks, holds through all nature:

> Tame animals have a better nature than wild, and all tame animals are better off when they are ruled by men, for then they are preserved. The male is by nature superior, and the female inferior; and the one rules and the other is ruled; this principle of necessity extends to all mankind. Nature would like to distinguish between the bodies of freemen and slaves; but this does not hold universally.

So the string of assertions goes on, and the discussion closes:

> It is clear, *therefore*, that some men are by nature free and others slaves, and that for these latter slavery is both expedient and right.

Having thus justified slavery to his own satisfaction, Aristotle proceeds to deal with household management, which he subdivides into three parts: the rule of a master over slaves, of a father, and of a husband:

> A husband and a father rules over wife and children, both free, but the rule differs: over his children it is a royal, over his wife a constitutional rule. For, although there may be exceptions to the order of nature, the male is by nature fitter for command than the female, just as the elder and full-grown is superior to the younger and more immature.

To illustrate his point, Aristotle quotes the saying of Amasis and his foot-pan, a good story, although it does not exactly strengthen the philosopher's position. Amasis was a commoner, who became King of Egypt; to prove to his subjects the essential equality of all matter, he had his metal bath melted down and re-cast as a statue, to which all the people made humble obeisance, although they had treated the foot-pan with contempt. Then Amasis drew his moral: the substance of both bath and statue is the same; there is merely a difference in outward form. 'Of this kind,' says Aristotle, 'is the relation between male and female; but there *the inequality is permanent.*'

It is the business of household management to ensure excellence, and we are faced at once by a difficulty: can a slave possess virtue? If he has virtue, in what will he differ from a freeman? A similar question may be raised about women and children: ought a woman to be called temperate, brave, and just? Aristotle solves the difficulty thus:

> Women and slaves have a sort of virtue, the virtue of the irrational part of the soul. The slave has no deliberate faculty at all; the woman has it, but with her it is inconclusive. The ruler must have moral virtue in perfection; the subject requires only that measure of virtue which is proper to him. Virtue will be common to man and woman, but it will not be the same virtue: *e.g.*, the courage of a man is shown in commanding, of a woman in obeying.

These are hard sayings, and they bring Aristotle into direct conflict with Plato, who, in the *Meno*, discusses the question whether the virtue of a man and a woman is the same or different, and comes to the conclusion that it is the same. But Aristotle never hesitates to criticise his former teacher, and it is a curious point how far his low estimate of women is not the result of the pupil's unconscious reaction against a master's enthusiasm. A great part of the *Politics* is, in fact, a criticism of the *Republic*, and the discussion on slavery, which occupies most of the first book, is followed by a close consideration of Plato's communistic State. The objections raised are of a severely practical nature, *e.g.*:

If the women are shared in common, and private property is retained, the men will see to the fields; but who will see to the house?

And again:

Two virtues are destroyed in the communistic State; first, temperance towards women (for it is an honourable action to abstain from another man's wife for temperance' sake); secondly, liberality in the matter of property. The legislation of such a State may have a specious appearance of benevolence, but such evils as there are in property are due to a cause that laws cannot eradicate: the wickedness of human nature. Indeed, we see that there is much more quarrelling among those who have all things in common, though there are not many of them, than there is among the vast majority of men who keep to private property.

The criticism, however, although acute on points of detail, does not touch the essentials of feminism, and, in the *Politics*, Aristotle often reveals himself unconsciously as Plato's former disciple. His remarks on education are based very largely, although he makes no acknowledgment, on his master's teaching and scarcely harmonise with his own views on women. The concluding sentences of the first book, for example, are distinctly Platonic in their tone:

The relations of husband and wife, parent and child, their several virtues, what in their intercourse with one another is good and what is evil, and how we may pursue the good and escape the evil, will have to be discussed when we speak of the different forms of government. For inasmuch as every family is a part of a State, and these relationships are the parts of a family, the virtue of the part must have regard to the virtue of the whole. And therefore women and children must be trained by education with an eye to the State, if the virtues of either of them are supposed to make any difference in the virtues of the State. And they must make a difference; for the children grow up to be citizens, and half the free persons in a State are women.

So in discussing the Spartan constitution he says:

A husband and a wife being each a part of every family, the State may be considered as about equally divided into men and women: and, therefore, in those States where the condition of the women is bad, half the city may be regarded as having no laws*—

a sentiment taken, with a slight difference of application, directly from Plato himself, and the Platonic influence is plainly seen in all the chapters which treat of marriage and education:

Since the legislator should begin by considering how the frames of the children whom he is rearing may be as good as possible, his first care will be about marriage, at what age should his citizens marry, and who are fit to marry.

So the discussion starts reasonably enough, but the conclusion hardly agrees with modern ideas of eugenics:

Women should marry when they are about eighteen years of age, and men at seven-and-thirty; then they

* *Politics*, 2, 9.

are in the prime of life, and the decline in the powers of both will coincide. Furthermore, the children, if their birth takes place at the time that may reasonably be expected, will succeed in their prime, when the fathers are already in the decline of life and have nearly reached their term of three-scores years and ten.

Aristotle here seems to be following not any ideal system, but the actual practice of his time, a practice which Euripides (fr. 319) had already condemned. The gap in age between husband and wife is far too great for any real physical or moral companionship. The husband, moreover, remaining unmarried until the age of thirty-seven, can hardly be supposed to have escaped from the illicit connections which were allowed and encouraged by Athenian custom: to say that such an one is in his prime is surely to mis-state the case. The art of being a grandfather also under this system tends to disappear, for a man could hardly hope to see grandchildren of his own, if neither he nor his sons married till they were thirty-seven: his daughters, of course, as Euripides again tells us (fr. 320), on marriage passed altogether out of their father's life. The whole arrangement is obviously wrong, but it suited the conditions of Athenian domestic life, where a young wife could be more easily kept in subjection and large families were neither desired nor customary; and because it existed, therefore to Aristotle it seemed right.

The female, found to be inferior in a moral and political sense, is also considered by Aristotle to be physically inferior to the male, and in the treatise *On Generation* he deals with this question frequently and at some length :

> Male and female differ in their essence by each having a separate ability or faculty, and anatomically by certain parts ; essentially the male is that which is able to generate in another, the female is that which is able to generate in itself and out of which comes into being the offspring previously existing in the parent.*

The distinction of sex is a first principle :

> An animal is not male or female in virtue of an isolated part or an isolated faculty : when that which distinguishes male and female suffers change many other changes accompany it, as would be the case if a first principle is changed.†

The treatise is concerned chiefly with the phenomena of reproduction :

> For the business of most animals is, you may say, nothing else than to produce young, as the business of a plant is to produce seed and fruit.‡

Sex-characteristics accordingly are described mainly in accordance with their reproductive functions.

As regards the origin of sex and the causes of male

* *De Generatione*, 716, a, 18. † *Ibid.* 716, b. 10.
‡ *Ibid.* 717, a, 20.

and female, Aristotle is a curious mixture of prejudice and insight. He begins thus :

> To suppose that heat and cold are the causes of male and female, or that the different sexes come from the right and left, is not altogether unreasonable in itself, for the right of the body is hotter than the left.

With him it is an unquestioning belief that the right is, in nature, superior to the left, the upper to the lower, the front to the back ; and nature, when no more important purpose stands in the way, places the more honourable part in the more honourable position. So it is that the heart, which is the nobler organ, is in the upper part of the body, while the stomach is in the lower. As he is equally sure that the male is superior to the female, the male elements in reproduction will come from the right or noble part of the body.

But the part taken by the male and female elements in the process of generation is, according to Aristotle, absolutely different. The child is not formed from a mixture of both, but the female contributes the material, the male is the active agent. The analogy used is that of a bed : the female is the wood, the male the carpenter, who, from the wood, makes the bed. The female is passive, the male is active :

> It is through a certain incapacity that the female is female : females are weaker and colder in nature

than males, and we must look upon the female character as being a sort of natural deficiency.*

Women, in Aristotle's view, are rather plants than animals; for the animal differs from the plant, chiefly in having sense-perception. If the sensitive soul is not present, the body is no better than a corpse, and this sensitive soul is supplied only by the male. The female provides the material, the male fashions it; the body is from the female, the soul from the male, who can stand outside the body just as the artist stands outside his creation. It certainly seems that female children progress more quickly than male, but that is merely a proof of their inferiority; for all inferior things come sooner to their perfection or end, and as this is true of works of art so it is true of what is formed by nature.

These quotations will illustrate that curious depreciation of the female element in nature and especially in man which is one of the weaker points in the treatise. It is continually recurring; for example, in describing the hair of animals these are the reasons given for baldness:

> The front part of the head goes bald because the brain is there and man is the only animal to go bald, because his brain is much the largest and moistest. *Women do not go bald.*†

* *De Generatione*, 728 a. † *Ibid*, 784, a.

So in the discussion of voice we read :

The voice of the female is higher than that of the male in all animals, and in man this is especially noticeable. A deep note is *better* than a high pitched : depth belongs to the nobler nature, and depth of tone shows a sort of superiority.*

Nor is this view of the physical, and consequently the mental, inferiority of the female confined to the *De Generatione* : it permeates the *History of Animals*, and finds its clearest expression there in a passage which perhaps gives the ultimate reason of Aristotle's error :

In all genera in which the distinction of male and female is found, Nature makes a similar differentiation in the mental characteristics of the two sexes. This differentiation is the most obvious in the case of human-kind and in that of the larger animals and the viviparous quadrupeds. In the case of these latter the female is softer in character, is the sooner tamed, admits more readily of caressing, and is more apt in the way of learning. With all animals, except the bear and the leopard, the female is softer in disposition than the male, is more mischievous, less simple, more impulsive, and more attentive to the nurture of the young. The traces of these differentiated characteristics are more or less visible in every species, but they are especially visible where character is the more developed, and most of all in man. The fact is, the nature of man is the most rounded off and complete, and consequently in man the qualities above referred to are found in

* *De Generatione*, 787, a.

their perfection. Hence woman is more compassionate than man, more easily moved to tears, at the same time is more jealous, more querulous, more apt to scold. She is, furthermore, more prone to despondency and less hopeful than the man, more void of shame or self-respect, more false of speech, more deceptive, and of more retentive memory. She is also more wakeful, more shrinking, more difficult to rouse to action, and requires a smaller quantity of nutriment.*

The Athenian women of the fourth century were the women that Aristotle knew best, and, given Aristotle's character and scientific method, it is not surprising that he should judge Woman in the abstract to be an inferior animal. If he had been a little more of a poet and idealist—in other words, if he had not been Aristotle—he might have taken another view; but considering the facts of Athenian life in his day, and Aristotle's disposition to cling to facts, we need not wonder at his estimate. The real mischief—and Aristotle's influence in this matter has been an enormous hindrance to human progress —was done not by the philosopher himself, for in his time the position of women could hardly have been altered for the worse, but by his blind followers in later ages when his slightest word was regarded almost as inspired truth. Aristotle himself is never dogmatic (he leaves that to weaker men), and does not profess to give anything but the some-

* *Hist. An.*, 608, b (trans. Thompson).

what casual expression of his own personal knowledge and opinions.

It is hardly right to blame him: women in his time undoubtedly were the inferior sex, and Aristotle is always the prophet of things as they are. The *protégé* of the absolute monarchy which had overthrown the city-states, he has no belief in abstract freedom or in social reform. For him, what is is right. 'Women and slaves are inferior,' he says to himself, 'by the conditions of existence as I see them: *therefore* they are inferior by the laws of nature,' and although he knows that this inferiority was the result of the conditions of their life, his business is only with facts.

But he generalises from insufficient data: Woman for him means the women of his time, and although he points out the influence of environment, he fails to distinguish between innate and accidental characteristics. And so again, in treating of the female sex in nature, he is too inclined to confine himself to the higher mammals. He emphasises the case of the herbivorous animals, those that go in herds, and are polygamous in their habits: deer, for example, where the male has a distinct advantage in size and strength; while he says little of the carnivora, who hunt in pairs and are monogamous, where the female tends to be equal in every respect to the male. Insects he almost disregards, and the microscope, in the hands of a naturalist of genius like M. Fabre, has opened up for us a world from which Aristotle was debarred by the material limitations of his instruments.

We see now that Nature, at least, has no favoured sex, and that Euripides' words are as true in a zoological as they are in a sociological sense: 'All that can be said of the male can be said equally well of the female, and *vice versa.*' The male that in some species is the stronger and more active, in others is the weaker and plays a passive rôle. The female mantis that devours her feeble mate is the reverse side of Nature's picture. So again, all the fascinating problems of parthenogenesis, whereby the female may produce for several births without the intervention of the male, have received a new light from the close study of the hive. Aristotle's chapter on bees suffers materially from lack of first-hand knowledge, and, as Professor Platt says, although it is greatly to his credit for hard thinking, it reveals the fact that he knew next to nothing about the subject. Of course, the whole method of bee-generation is totally at variance with Aristotle's theory of male superiority, and if he had possessed our knowledge his theory might have been modified. In the world of insects, at least, feminism reigns; the male is weak and subservient, the female is the ruler. Often the male is an accident;

the female would have sufficed. So true is this that a modern essayist, M. Remy de Gourmont, writing under the influence of Fabre's discoveries, can vary Aristotle's analogy and compare the female to the clock and the male to the necessary key that winds up the mechanism.

But although Aristotle can scarcely be said to understand all the mysteries of sex, he anticipates some of the most fruitful investigations of modern research, and in all questions of pure science, within the limits of his own experience, he is almost infallible. It is unfortunate that his experience of women was misleading, and that the problems of feminism do not always fall within the confines of science. That he was wrong in this matter is chiefly the fault of his times and their social conditions, and those who live in other days and amid other surroundings should remember his own significant words, spoken indeed about bees, but equally applicable to other social animals :

> Such appears to me to be the truth, judging from theory and what I believe to be the facts. But up to the present the facts have not been sufficiently comprehended ; if ever they are, then credit must be given to observation rather than to theories, and to theories only if what they affirm agrees with observed facts.

And with that quotation we may well leave him : *Amicus Aristoteles; magis amica veritas.* If the facts of modern existence show women to be the inferior sex, then, and then only, are we moderns justified in holding that opinion. But every man should judge for himself on the evidence that his own observation gives, and not be influenced by the theories of other men or by the literature of the past.

In Aristotle's time, for reasons which this brief survey of Greek literature has, perhaps, made plain, the facts of women's nature were certainly not sufficiently comprehended. Euripides and Plato are almost the only authors who show any true appreciation of a woman's real qualities, and to Euripides and Plato, Aristotle, by the whole trend of his prejudices, was opposed. His mistake was that he failed to realise the moral aspects of feminism. A nation that degrades its women will inevitably suffer degradation itself. Aristotle lent the weight of his name to a profound error, and helped to perpetuate the malady which had already been the chief cause of the destruction of Greece.

For Product Safety Concerns and Information please contact our EU representative GPSR@taylorandfrancis.com
Taylor & Francis Verlag GmbH, Kaufingerstraße 24, 80331 München, Germany

www.ingramcontent.com/pod-product-compliance
Lightning Source LLC
Chambersburg PA
CBHW070528100726
47907CB00004B/1029

* 9 7 8 1 0 3 2 8 2 8 2 1 3 *